7 Steps to Effective Time Management

Prem P. Bhalla

GOODWILL PUBLISHING HOUSE®
B-3 RATTAN JYOTI, 18 RAJENDRA PLACE
NEW DELHI-110008 (INDIA)

Published by
GOODWILL PUBLISHING HOUSE®
B-3 Rattan Jyoti, 18 Rajendra Place
New Delhi-110008 (INDIA)
Tel. : 25750801, 25820556
Fax : 91-11-25764396
E-mail : goodwillpub@vsnl.net
website : www.goodwillpublishinghouse.com

Printed at :
Kumar Offset, Delhi

Contents

Preface

Time is God's gift to us. He gives it to everyone without attaching any pre-conditions for its usage. Some use it well. However, a vast majority just let it fritter away, not realising that time does not wait for anyone. It flows like a perennial river. We only know that it flows from the future, and recedes into the past. Every individual has been given a limited number of years, months and days to experience it.

For time, everyone is alike. It makes no distinctions between individuals, their caste, colour or creed. It does not care where a person lives, or what religion or faith one follows. It gives equally to all, to the rich and the poor. It keeps flowing at its steady speed, neither too fast, nor too slow. It never changes its pace. If individuals think that sometimes "time hangs heavy" and at other times "it flows too fast", the difference lies in the minds of the people, who think this way. Time flows at its usual pace.

The proper utilisation of time is a matter of concern to all conscientious people. They appreciate that time is a capital, and not an income. No one can have more or less of it. Like any capital, it is precious. We must use it to the best of our ability. Initially, we can use this capital to acquire personal skills and abilities, and later utilise it for our personal benefit at home, at the workplace and in the society.

This book aims at taking you step by step to understand the qualities of time better. It explains that to get the best from the time granted to us in this lifetime, we should not try to manage time, but manage our own lives better to attain more, with lesser effort, in the same time. This becomes easy when we evaluate our personal attitude and use of time, and also understand how common everyday activities cheat us of productivity. Adoption of positive habits lead a person to useful time management skills and a more effective life.

— Prem P. Bhalla

Step 1 Get to Know Time

What is time? What does it mean to you? Few can respond to these questions immediately, because we never think of it in that light. Yet, the word is used every day in a variety of ways.

What time is it? Oh, what a waste of time? What time does the flight depart? I am just killing time. What time should we meet? This is the first time that I have come alone. Were they able to take advantage of the extra time? What time did he record to complete the race? This is the best time to rest. I am fighting against time. You have reached here ahead of time. For the time being, I will accept what you give. This work is very time consuming.

These are only a few sentences that use the word 'time' to make statements, or ask questions. To these we could add many more. However, it would be difficult to define time just by reading these sentences. There is much more to it.

WHAT DOES TIME MEAN?

The Random dictionary defines time as indefinite continuous duration regarded as that in which events succeed one another. It is also defined as finite duration, or a period or interval, as between two events. For example: *We have met after a long time*. It also means a system or method of measuring or reckoning the passage of time. It also refers to a particular period considered as distinct from other periods. For example: *The period after retirement is the best time to do things you always wanted to do.* Time also means a prescribed or allotted period, as of one's life, or for payment of debt. For example: *Youth is a time for education and preparation for adult life. I will give you a month's time to return my money.* It can also refer to a period with reference to personal experience. For example: *We had a very good time at the hill resort.* One definition that is easy to understand is a particular or definite point of time as indicated by the clock. For example: *What time is it?*

The Webster's dictionary defines time briefly as duration, era, period, age; space of time at one's disposal; season; proper time; rhythm.

The Oxford dictionary defines time as the unlimited continued progress of existence and events in the past, present and future, regarded as a whole. It is also described as a point of time as measured in hours and minutes past midnight, or noon. For example: *The time is 10.00 a.m., or 10.00 p.m.* It also means the right or agreed moment to do something. For example: *This is the right time to leave.* Or, *The departure time of the flight is 11.25 a.m.* Time also refers to the length of time taken to complete an activity. For example: *You must include the time taken to get off the flight and collect the baggage before one reaches the exit gate.* When one talks of 'a time', it means an indefinite period.

TIME AND OTHER WORDS

The word 'time' is used in conjunction with a lot of other words, giving it many special meanings. For example, *time frame* refers to a specified period of time. *Time honoured* refers to a custom or tradition respected or valued because it has existed for a long time. *Timekeeper* is a person who is punctual. It also refers to a person who records the amount of time taken by a process, or activity, one who keeps the time of workmen. It can also mean a clock, a watch or other instrument. *Timepiece* also means an instrument for measuring time. A *timer* is an automatic mechanism for operating a device at a preset time. It also refers to a person or device that records the time taken by a process or activity.

Time bomb is a bomb designed to explode at a set time. *Time capsule* is a container in which a selection of objects typical of the present time is buried for discovery in the future. *Time lapse* is used to describe a photographic technique taking a sequence of frames at set intervals to record changes that take place slowly over time.

Time sheet is a piece of paper for recording the number of hours worked. A *time card* is a card used to record the time of arrival and departure at work. *Time-server* is a person who makes little effort at work because he or she is waiting to leave or retire. A *timetable* is a list or plan of times at which events are scheduled to take place. *Timeshare* is an arrangement in which joint owners use a property as a holiday home at different specified times.

The word 'time' has been used in many other ways. For example, *timely* refers to something done or occurring at a good and appropriate time. When something is unaffected by the passage of time, or by changes in fashion, it is referred to as *timeless.* The time that is spent away from one's usual work or studies is described as *time off. Time saving* refers to methods and devices that help reduce the time spent or required for an activity. On the other hand, *time consuming* refers to excessive wastage of time.

The word is also used to describe the use of time. While *time lag* refers to the period between two closely related events, *time-out* refers to an intermission, a break, or a brief suspension of activity. *Time immemorial* describes time in the distant past beyond memory or record. When a person is punctual, he or she is said to be *in time.* When the person is occupied in an activity to make time pass quickly, he or she is said to *kill time.* To *make time* means to move quickly to recover lost time. When progress of an activity is suspended temporarily it is described as to *mark time.*

When a person is slow or leisurely, he or she is said to *take one's time. Time of life* refers to age. For example: *At your time of life, you must be careful about your health. Time after time* means something done repeatedly. From *time to time* means something done occasionally. Whereas *ahead of time* refers to before the due time, *behind the times* means old fashioned or dated. *For the time being* means as at present. It also means temporarily. *Against time* refers to an effort to finish an activity within a limited time.

TIME, MUSIC AND RHYTHM

The word 'time' is also used to describe the rhythmic pattern or tempo of a piece of music. When two or more singers make a presentation, and one is not in harmony, he or she is said to be *out of time.* In the same way, in an outdoor parade if a person does not march in unison with the rest, he or she is said to be *out of time.* This way, we notice that time, rhythm and harmony are connected. When a person learns to be in harmony with time, it would be the first step to learning effective time management.

> **Think it over...**
>
> Desire to have things done quickly prevents their being done thoroughly.
>
> — *Confucius*

POPULAR PHRASES ABOUT TIME

Yet another way to learn more about time is to examine the many popular phrases used in everyday conversation about time. A few are described here.

- **Stand the tests of time**: to be popular and in use even after a long time has gone by.
- **Play for time**: to delay an action or event until the conditions improve for the individual.
- **Take one's time**: to not hurry up, or to do something at one's own speed.
- **Half the time**: most of the time.
- **All in good time**: soon, when it is the right time.
- **At one time**: some time in the past.
- **Do time**: serve a sentence in prison.

- **Ahead of one's time**: to have ideas that is in advance of current thinking, and often not understood.
- **A stitch in time saves nine**: prompt action at the sight of a problem that does not permit the situation to get worse.
- **Have the time of one's life**: to have an enjoyable time.
- **In good time**: early enough, with some time to spare.
- **Have time on one's hand**: to have more time than is necessary for an activity.
- **Make good time**: to have a journey as rapidly as expected.
- **In the nick of time**: to be just in time as though at the last moment.
- **Have a thin time of it**: to have an unpleasant or difficult time.
- **Have no time for (someone or something)**: to have a low opinion about someone or something, and to wish not to associate with the person or thing.
- **Time is getting on**: time is passing, and it is getting late.
- **Time flies**: time passes very quickly.
- **Time and time again**: repeatedly.
- **No time at all**: a very short time.
- **In one's own good time**: at one's personal convenience.

- **In the fullness of time**: when the appropriate time has come.
- **Hit the big time**: to attain great success and fame.
- **Take time by the forelock**: to act quickly and without delay.

SIMILAR WORDS

There are several words similar to the word 'time'. It is worthwhile to be acquainted with them. These words include age, date, duration, epoch, era, interim, period, season, span, spell, tempo and term. The more we understand how time is linked with different situations, the better we can plan the use of time.

TIME AND THE INDIVIDUAL

From the foregoing paragraphs it is evident how closely every individual is linked with time. The many words, the phrases and the sentences about time reflect the attitude of people about what they feel about time. Some look at it from a positive angle, but there are others who sometimes need to "kill time".

Every individual is a complex human being, but the way people look at and utilise their time can tell you much not only about what they say or do, but also about their personal attitude, their family, their way of working, and how they conduct their life in public.

Time affects individuals in many ways. The physical impact of time influences how they schedule their everyday activities, and also how they look at the past and future. Simultaneously, time exerts a psychological impact in that every passing moment exerts pressures on the mind when time is not utilised according to set schedules. The interaction with time influences an individual's outlook towards life, creating a philosophical impact, when one adopts or contradicts traditional guidelines like *Time and tide wait for no man*. Few realise it that time also has a biological impact on individuals. This is important as it affects individual productivity, and is discussed in greater detail later.

Time is a valuable asset. It is important how everyone reacts to its influences and utilizes it. Ultimately, the individual's attitude about time gives an insight into the person's character.

TIME AND MONEY

When one talks of time, a popular statement made by many people is *Time is money*. Even to a labourer, who offers his physical labour, time is money. If he does not reach the workplace in time, he is refused work. No work means no money. If he works half a day, he gets paid only half the wages. If he were to work extra hours, he would receive a proportionately higher wage. We could equate all kinds of workers with a labourer. They receive money and other amenities on the basis of the days of active work they put in.

Office workers may not be doing physical work, but they too receive their wages and salaries on the basis of the time they put in each day, week and month. Instead of physical work, these workers offer clerical and office skills. The income is directly proportional to the time they put into their work.

The managerial staff offers their management skills for the money they receive. Their skills are rated higher in terms of work done each day, or even each hour, but their emoluments are certainly linked with the time they spend at work. Along with the abilities, the name, or the brand value of an individual affects the earning value of an individual. At the highest level, when making comparisons, people are known to work out the earning capacity of an individual every minute. This shows how important it is to put in one's very best efforts to be productive, and generate as high an income as is possible each day.

At every level of work, income is linked with the time and effort one puts into his or her vocation each day. This motivates most people to work longer and harder. However, it has been seen that different individuals may put in the same number of hours at work, but some of them have a higher productivity in comparison with their colleagues. This can be due to better skills and working techniques, but amongst people with similar skills, those who manage their time better are more efficient, and also enjoy greater leisure and freedom from stress.

Think it over...

Nothing great is created suddenly, any more than a bunch of grapes or a fig. If you tell me that you desire a fig, I answer you that there must be time. Let it first blossom, then bear fruit, then ripen.

— *Epictetus*

TIME AND DEATH

Few like to think that way, but time is also linked with death. Everyone is born with a limited life span. At the same time, everyone has a limited working life, with the government and several other organisations having adopted retirement norms for individuals. Death is the ultimate destination for all living beings. From the day one is born, with each passing day, time is carrying every individual towards death. This is the reality even though we do not like to think in this manner. Rather than feel sorry for the reducing life span, one celebrates the birthday each year as a landmark attained. This should really be a day of gratitude for having been blessed with the grace of God. When we think in terms of time and death being linked, we are reminded that every individual has a limited amount of time at his or her command. It is rightly said that time and tide wait for no one. Therefore, it is very important that whatever time is available must be utilised in the best manner. This is possible only with good time management.

Think it over...

Time is the chariot of all ages to carry men away.

— *Francesco Petrarch*

WHAT IS TIME?

We need to understand time and its attributes a little better. After all, what is time? How does it affect us in everyday life?

Time is God's gift to us. He does not shower the same span of life to everyone. Some are more blessed than others. Like any other gift, we need to be grateful to God for whatever time He has given us. In response, we should resolve to put God's gift to the best use.

Time is a capital. It is not an income. We have no hand in having more or less of it. As a capital, it is for us to either invest it well, or let it fritter away. Like any capital, it is precious. We must use it to the best of our ability. Initially, we need to utilise this capital to acquire personal abilities and skills, and later on to use it for the welfare of our families, for generating income at our workplace, and to develop the community where we live. That would be the only way to use the capital correctly.

Time is ever flowing like a perennial river. We have never seen its source. Perhaps like all other gifts of Nature, God controls it. We only know that it flows from the future and recedes to the past. Every individual has been given only a limited number of years, months and days to experience it. God has given everyone the freedom to decide how one wishes to utilise it. There is no hindrance or compulsion upon us. Whether one benefits by its use, or lets it just fritter away is a personal choice.

For time, everyone is alike. It makes no distinctions between individuals, their caste, colour or creed. It does not care where a person lives, or what religion one follows. It gives equally to all. Like a river, time does not wait for anyone. It keeps flowing at its steady speed, neither too fast, nor too slow. It never changes its pace. If individuals think that sometimes "time hangs heavy" and at other times, "it flows too fast", the difference lies in the minds of the people who think this way. Time keeps flowing at its fixed pace. It has been doing this since times immemorial.

A river can be obstructed with a barrage or a dam, and the water stored for future use. However, time just keeps flowing. Its flow cannot be obstructed. Neither can it be stored for future use. There is no substitute for time.

It cannot be replaced with anything. Time is time, and will remain so forever.

Time is inelastic. We cannot use it in phases. It must be used as it comes. Every year has 365¼ days. Every day has 24 hours, every hour has 60 minutes, and each minute has 60 seconds. This is so for everyone, both the rich and the poor.

Time is a willing partner. It accepts whatever a person does. There are no free samples of time to experiment with. If some time is lost, the experience can be a useful lesson to learn the better utilisation of time.

Considering the many attributes of time, it is common for people to link time with money. When we do it, we find that time is expensive. For a person earning one lakh rupees a year it means almost Rs 1 for every minute. This motivates people to work longer and to put in more effort.

Busy people put time to best use. They have time for everyone – the family, at the workplace and the society. It seems that they have time for everything. The fact is that they are efficient. They know how to utilise the time best through good time management.

> **Think it over...**
>
> What is time? – The shadow on the dial, the striking of the clock, the running of the sand, day and night, summer and winter, months, years, centuries – these are but the arbitrary and outward signs – the measure of time, not time itself. Time is the life of the soul.
>
> — *Longfellow*

TIME AND BIORHYTHMS

Simply stated, biorhythm refers to a recurring cycle in the functioning of an organism, such as the daily cycle of keeping awake and sleeping. We cannot ignore that each day, as time flows, we experience a day and night. Over a longer period we also experience the changes in weather and climates affecting not only human beings, but also the plant and animal life.

Biorhythms reflect rhythmic change, caused by hormones, in the physical state and activity patterns of plants and animals affected by seasonal changes. These cause hibernation and affect breeding and migratory patterns in animals, and spring flowering in a variety of plants. The hormonal changes are caused by the variation in the length of the day (photo periodism). These changes communicate the time of the year to the plants and animals.

The circadian rhythm affecting the metabolic rhythm is based on the changes in the 24-hour day, and is found in most living beings. The sleeping and waking patterns depend upon it. At the same time, the body temperature and the moods also follow a set rhythm. In sick people, the body temperature, blood pressure and the pulse are recorded at fixed times each day to observe these changes. These changes can be observed clearly when a person travels swiftly in a jet plane into areas with different timings, and sleeping and waking patterns. The biological changes are described as 'jet lag', and it takes some time before the body gets adjusted to the new environments and timings.

The importance of understanding the relationship between time and biorhythms in individuals is that at different times of the day these affect the efficiency. At certain times individuals perform more efficiently than at other times. Taking advantage of this fact, the more difficult and challenging assignments can be handled when the efficiency is at a peak, and the routine jobs can be handled at other times. This ensures high productivity and good time management.

TIME AND CULTURAL DIFFERENCES

People around the world have different working styles and patterns. These are in conformity with the cultural patterns of the region or country. These are often conditioned by the attitude of the local residents and the prevalent climate and weather conditions. For example, the people in developed countries adhere strictly to time, leaving home around 8.00 a.m. and returning by 6.00 p.m. Even the shops in the markets follow a strict time schedule, closing latest by 7.00 p.m. The working times in developing countries are different, with many establishments beginning work late, and also closing work at late hours. The shops in the market may also remain open until late. In some countries, there is also a provision for an afternoon siesta, particularly in the hot summer months.

The cultural differences reflect in attitudes about punctuality at social events and community functions. At religious get-togethers there may be no control over time sometimes. This can be a difficult situation for the person who believes in punctuality and good time management. A callous attitude about time can result at loss of hundreds of man-hours at a single function. This can cause a lot of frustration amongst time-conscious people.

With wide-scale globalisation of business, it is important to understand how cultural differences affect attitudes and utilization of time. This knowledge can help in developing practices that make good time management possible.

IS TIME A FRIEND OR FOE?

Having understood how time plays a significant part in the lives of all people, and also how individuals perceive different attributes of time, you need to take a new look at time. Do you consider it a friend, or a foe? If you are able to handle your many responsibilities towards your family, your children, at the workplace and in the society where you live, comfortably without undue pressures of time, you have every reason to consider time your friend. You are making the best use of time.

However, most people are not so fortunate. They begin their day early, and end it late. They spend the least amount of time with the family. Only the very urgent responsibilities towards the society are fulfilled. These people are forever short of time. The pressure is only building up. How long they can cope up with the pressure is not known. One cannot also predict whether the final outcome would be good, unpleasant or even disastrous. We meet young people who are burnt-out as early as in the thirties. There is a silver lining to the dark clouds that appear gloomy. There still is hope for these young people. They can learn to organise their lives better. More than anything else, they can adopt good time management techniques to achieve more in less time, and enjoy more of leisure time to recharge for still greater challenges.

Think it over...

Time is what we want most, but what alas we use worst.

— *Penn*

TIME IN EVERYDAY LIFE

The time in the everyday life of a person can be divided broadly into personal time and working time. The personal time can again be further divided into time for common human needs and discretionary time. We need to understand the various components of these subdivisions.

The time for common human needs includes time for sleep, for bathing, dressing and an occasional visit to the barber or beauty saloon. The time for travel to work could also be included in this category.

The time spent at work is important because it reflects individual productivity. It is customary to spend a minimum of 8 hours at work almost all over the world, but how productively every person uses this time decides how high he or she can rise. The self-employed persons tend to spend more time at work.

The discretionary time includes the time spent with the family, with friends, and also that spent in helping with the household work, or used in leisure activities like watching the TV.

With the breakdown of everyday time of 24 hours into various components, a person can appreciate whether he or she is utilising the time well. If not, one can still learn to understand where the time is wasted, and also how this wastage can be avoided and personal productivity enhanced.

LONG-TERM VIEW OF TIME

Life has to be lived one day at a time, broken further into 24 hours. However, time does not flow in units of one day each. Days add on to make a week, and weeks add on to make a month. Months make a year. Years together make a life. Since seasons vary over the years, individual productivity too varies over different times of the weeks and months, it becomes necessary not only to understand and plan for the 24-hour day, but to plan ahead for weeks, months and years. Everyone needs to plan for short-term and long-term goals. We will consider these at a later stage.

> **Think it over...**
>
> What then is time? If no one asks me, I know; if I want to explain it to a questioner, I do not know.
>
> — *St. Augustine*

POINTS TO PONDER

- Time is the unlimited continued progress of existence and events in the past, present and future, regarded as a whole.
- Time is linked with many words to describe a variety of experiences and meanings.
- Time has inspired a large number of popular phrases.

- To the busy man time is money.
- Few realise it that time is carrying everyone towards death.
- Time is God's gift to everyone.
- Time affects both plant and animal life.
- The attitude about time reflects how one uses it.
- Time can be both, a friend and a foe.
- We need to take a short-term as well as a long-term view of time.

Step 2

The Management

Everyone feels that he or she is using personal time in the best possible way. However, experience has shown that it is not so. There is much that can be done. Fortunately, everyone can learn to improve upon one's performance through good time management.

Time management, in simple terms, is the use of methods to increase personal and corporate productivity through better utilisation of time. It includes ways to plan everyday activities, set goals and work on the basis of set priorities. It is doing what is necessary at the right place and at the appropriate time.

Since everyone is responsible for the use of his or her time to personal benefit, good time management is based upon discipline and self-management. To achieve this, one draws strength from cultivating good personal and working habits. The techniques are simple and useful, but can be learnt only through consistent effort. It must necessarily begin with the desire to put the time to best use.

TIME CONSCIOUSNESS

You cannot manage your time well unless you are conscious about the characteristics of time. We have already discussed them. Study them once again. Time is a great resource. It is for you to put it to best use. Since it is related to your attitude about time, it begins with your thought processes. If you are casual about time, it only means that you lack the value of time, and are not time conscious.

Those who wish to get ahead through greater productivity cannot afford to be casual about the utilisation of time. They know that once the time is gone, it will never return. It is a wasting resource. If not utilised, it is lost forever. The only thing you can gain from lost time is experience – of things that do, or do not work. To become time conscious, you must accept time as a valuable but limited resource, and have not only a watch on your wrist, but clocks in your home and office to remind you of the minutes and hours ticking away into eternity. Use time as a working guide. You will learn to be more productive and time conscious. You would step into the world of better time management.

TIME MANAGEMENT IS...

People often ask: How does one manage time? The truth is that you do not manage time. You manage your life in relation to time.

Good time management leads a person to a more relaxed life, free from fatigue and stress. Fatigue and stress are holding back millions of young people from getting ahead in a competitive world. It is not possible to take competition away from everyday life. It has come to stay. However, it is possible to keep a check on fatigue and stress and avoid an early burnout caused by them. Physical fatigue is easily recognised, as it follows strenuous work. Emotional fatigue is not easy to understand or recognise. It builds up slowly, and gradually causes what is popularly known as stress or tension. It goes on to create physical and emotional problems, and is known to create hell in the lives of many ambitious young people. Planned management of time can help solve this problem.

A relaxed person always works effectively. The secret of greater productivity and success does not lie in working hard, or in being efficient or perfect. Success comes from correct planning, and the aim to be effective in achieving whatever one sets out to do.

To be effective, it would be necessary to work out one's own rules, and not be tied down to the traditional ways of doing things. Many young people insist that they are following what their father or grandfather did. If they were successful, why will we not be so? The truth is that what was right two or four decades away need not hold good today. It may be valid to a certain degree, but not completely. Much of the progress in the world came because there were people who dared to be different, and proved that they were right.

To get ahead, it is equally important that there should be local control, and not centralised control. Too much time is lost in seeking permissions and filing explanations and reports. When the control is local, there is greater effectiveness in every field of activity.

With effectiveness as the central criterion, the planning leads one not to short-term plans and work programmes, but to long-term goal setting. One does not think in terms of planning for the day or the week, but over the month, three months, annually and also over the next few years.

The goals inspire and challenge a person to continuously raise personal productivity.

With higher productivity and achievement, the greatest benefit comes as job satisfaction. The returns are higher. One is relaxed in day-to-day activities, enjoying more of leisure time. This can be used for personal growth and better family relationships. This, in turn, leads to greater creativity and ability to rise higher in life. This also leads to more positive attitude towards life and the utilisation of time. Good time management is, ultimately, having the correct attitudes towards the use of time.

Most people are very casual about their use of time. It is in their attitude. If they insist upon a casual attitude towards time, they cannot expect to be effective at home, at the workplace or in society. The moment they decide to change the attitude from casual to one that is focussed on what they do, they begin to become productive and effective. A positive attitude is a great self-motivating force. With greater motivation, one strives to learn new techniques to utilise time better.

Increased leisure time is the greatest benefit of good time management. With more leisure there is more time for planning and for creative activities. Besides, it gives one more time for personal use. This is very important because people tend to ignore their own needs to fulfil responsibilities towards the family, at the workplace and also for building better relationships in the community where they live. Good time management is a sure way to get ahead in every field of life.

TIME MANAGEMENT IS NOT...

Contrary to what most people feel, time management is not efficiency gone mad. Most people think time management means getting obsessed with being good and efficient all the time. They feel it is like being driven with an invisible whip represented by the hands of a clock. Others feel that time management drives everyone to the limit, pushing the workers almost against the wall. This is not true. Time management aims at creating a balance between what needs to be done and leisure. It is to know that life is more comfortable when it is organised intelligently.

Many feel that time management is a ruthless and selfish approach to life. They insist that it aims at working harder personally, and making others do so. Again, this is not correct. It does not aim at working *harder*. Instead, it aims at working *smarter*. Most people are not afraid of working harder. They are willing to put in extra effort. The important thing is to know where to put that extra effort to be more effective. One learns this through time management techniques.

Another wrong concept about time management is that it promotes a rigid and inflexible attitude towards what needs to be done. By doing so, it robs a person of his or her individuality, and also creativity. This is not so. In reality, time management aims at saving time from unnecessary activities, and adding it to the leisure time. This promotes greater relaxation and increases creativity rather than reducing it.

It must also be remembered that an efficient person is not necessarily a good time manager. One can be efficient, but may not be effective. Good time management stresses upon effectiveness, and not upon personal efficiency. Whereas to be efficient would mean to **do things right**, to be effective would mean to **do right things**.

Once a person can understand what time management is, and what it is not, the next obvious question is: Can time management be learnt?

LEARNING TIME MANAGEMENT

There are two ways of becoming a good time manager. The first one is to learn it through a systematic approach towards it. It is like learning any other skill. The second way is to learn it as you struggle through life, making mistakes and learning from them. This way the learning is uncertain, and comes in small doses the harder way. Some learn from their follies. Most prefer to blame their destiny and others for what they are.

Here are a few hard facts.

- Nobody is born a good time manager.
- The only way to becoming one is to learn about it.
- There are no shortcuts. You need to learn it just as you would learn any other skill.
- It cannot be learnt overnight. It will require persistent effort over a long period.
- People who come from disciplined families, or have studied in schools where great importance is given to discipline, learn faster.
- Those who insist that they do not need time management techniques are really closing their eyes to reality. They are building walls around them. This way they fail to take advantage of time.
- When a person decides to become a good time manager, it is a lifetime commitment to becoming an effective person.

- Good time management begins with an understanding of oneself, with personal motivation, and by being aware that it will promote greater productivity and personal fulfilment.

ATTITUDE ABOUT TIME

It is very important how a person feels about time. These feelings shape one's attitudes about time. These attitudes, in turn, influence how one utilises time.

Have you noticed that a dating couple holding hands and watching a movie come out saying that the movie was rather short? At the same time, another youngster, who would have preferred to be playing football, and was compelled to accompany the parents to the movie, would come out telling how long and boring the movie was. The same movie, running at one time, and yet the reactions differ, and contrary to each other. If others would be questioned, there would be many differing responses. The differences arise from personal attitudes about time.

The attitude of the people about time can be gauged from the way they talk about it. In the first step we saw how people talk about time. Let us look at some specific examples.

Many say, "The time just flew away." A time conscious person would have said, "I did not keep track of time."

Again, we hear many say, "The time was lost." A positive way to say the same thing could be, "I did not make the best use of time."

We have all heard, "Where has the time gone?" Would it not have been better to say, "How did I use the time?"

Very often we hear, "It was a waste of time." A good time manager would say, "I wasted much time."

Many would say, "It was an enjoyable pastime." But a time conscious manager would say, "It was enjoyable, but unproductive."

We may not accept it immediately, but good time management begins with the correct attitude towards time. We have all seen that while parents would send their children to school in time, because if they are late, the school authorities may not keep them. However, the same parents are not particular when they send the children late to birthday parties, or personally go late to meetings or weddings and other parties. It is all in the attitude. Just as we discussed earlier, one must develop time consciousness, but it is equally important that one must also learn to respect time – one's own and also of others. When we respect time, it will respect us by making us productive.

EARLY TEACHINGS

It would only be right to mention Frank Bunker Gilbreth (1868 – 1924), and his wife Lillian Moller Gilbreth, who were the pioneers of motion study. Together they studied the habits of factory workers to find out ways to increase their levels of productivity. They are credited to have refined the hand motions into 17 basic motions, which were named **therbligs**, which is Gilbreth spelled backwards with "th" transposed. Frank and Lillian were both scientists, who insisted that things should be questioned, and when a better way was found, the older concepts must be discarded.

Besides their pioneering work, the couple is remembered for two of the most remarkable achievements. The first was the induction of the surgical nurse to assist the surgeon, thereby bringing about speed and productivity in surgical operations. Frank compared her to a caddy. The second was to teach freshly inducted soldiers to be able to disassemble and reassemble their weapons blindfolded, or in total darkness. As can be appreciated, these two achievements are credited to have saved innumerable lives.

The .couple had a large family with eleven living children, and they researched and experimented with them. A son, Frank Jr. and daughter Ernestine together described the parent's work lovingly in their book *Cheaper by the Dozen*, which was made into a movie. Their second book *Belles on their Toes* was a sequel to their earlier book.

Although the two differed in their attitudes, the work of the Gilbreths is often compared with that of Frederick Winslow Taylor, who worked to cut down the time of different processes. However, it is agreed that while the Gilbreths focussed on the welfare of the workers by reducing the number of motions in an activity, Taylor worked to increase profit through increased productivity. Since then, time management has come a long way.

LATER DEVELOPMENTS

Over the years, time management is often related to working with goals or objectives defined clearly in writing, and then following them up through a well-designed **Plan of Action**.

In the more recent years, Stephen R. Covey has summed up the suggestions put forth by management gurus as the four generations of time management.

1. **Reminders:** This method restricts itself to keeping notes and making lists to serve as reminders. One uses these as guides to follow up activities. If something is left undone, it is transferred to the next list.
2. **Planning and preparation:** This method suggests the use of calendars and appointment books. Meetings are listed. Deadlines for different activities are also noted. This method moves on from using reminders to planning and preparation, which look into the future as goals to be achieved.
3. **Planning, Prioritising and Controlling:** This method moves on from planning to prioritising and control of the activities on time basis. There is special emphasis on working according to priorities.
4. **Being efficient and proactive:** Although planning continues to be important, the emphasis at this stage is on what is urgent, and what is important. The use of this concept is not easy because many activities together contribute towards a goal, and if some of the activities are avoided as being unimportant or less important, it may not be possible to achieve the goal as initially conceived at the planning stage.

WORKING TO PRIORITIES

The differentiation between what is urgent and what is important leads a person to working to priorities.

Choosing between different activities is not easy. This has lead to further thinking on the subject.

The **ABC analysis** aims at dividing data and activities into groups, each group called A, B, C or something down the line. The activities listed in the group A are most important, and those in subsequent groups represent the reducing importance as perceived by the analyst.

The larger companies that work on national or international level often categorise territories and cities and plan their manufacturing and selling in harmony with this analysis. For example, the metro cities may be marked A, state capitals as B, larger cities as C and smaller towns as D. This way, the sales staff's activities, the sales orders and product promotions are planned. This. In turn, increases the effectiveness of productivity of the company personnel.

An Italian economist Vilfredo Pareto (1848–1923) enunciated what is popularly known as the **Pareto Time Principle**. This principle simply states that within any system, some constituent elements yield higher returns than others, with 20 percent of the total elements yielding high returns that produce 80 percent of the work. The other 80 percent of the elements produce 20 percent of the work.

If we accept the Pareto Time Principle, it means that if on a particular day we have 10 things to do, and if we choose the two most important of the things to do, our productivity would be 80 percent. When we are able to do some of the other 8 things, our productivity would proportionately rise higher. The important problem before us then is to choose those two things that are most important, and also prioritise the other 8 so that our productivity increases.

The Pareto Time Principle can also be applied to the less desirable results. For example, 20 percent of the people in a meeting are likely to monopolise 80 percent of the time. It can also mean that 20 percent of the customers may bring in 80 percent of the complaints. The converse is also true.

Some management gurus are of the opinion that whereas the Time Principle holds, the ratio is not 20:80, but is rather 30:70. Some also insist that it could vary with the individual perception of problems. However, this Time Principle leads us to an important aspect of increasing personal productivity. It makes it obvious that it is not necessary to do everything, because it may not always be possible within the time available. The secret of increasing productivity lies in doing what is important. This immediately draws our attention to appreciate the need for prioritising all our activities. This is exactly what all successful managers do.

In 1955, Peter Drucker gave us the phrase: **Management by Objectives**. This has changed the mindset of managers all over the world. Setting objectives is to set targets or goals. Although some still object to this thinking on the grounds that setting objectives makes operations inflexible, they inhibit creativity, and in general are not in harmony with the job requirements or the personal temperament, most of the managers in every field of activity swear by it. They feel that nothing could increase productivity better than management by objectives. For convenience, the phrase has been abbreviated to MBO.

> **Think it over...**
>
> Goals provide a sense of direction and purpose.
>
> — *Goldstein*

GOAL SETTING

Setting goals is to know your destination. A person who does not know his destination is only moving. Neither the person, nor others, knows where he is going. A goal means that a person has a desired result to achieve. To shoot without a target would be like shooting in the air, hoping that the bullet will hit a bird. We know that it does not happen that way.

Without realising it, we have always been working with goals. We learnt goal setting in school. The teachers would spread out the syllabus over the teaching session so that they could cover the subject within the allocated time. It was equally important to equitably divide the time to cover all the subjects. Besides, it was important that we must prepare ourselves to cover the curriculum in one academic year, and move on to the next class. Unfortunately, while we remember the three Rs we learnt at school, we overlook the concepts that are used to teach us. We forget that we would not reach the class late for fear of being thrown out. We also forget that we had set goals before us to complete the work in one academic session. Is it not surprising that we need to be reminded about punctuality and working according to goals?

A goal is like a site plan for a building. Just as it is not possible for the architect to make the house of your dreams without a site plan giving details of various rooms and needs, it is not possible to achieve much without specific goals in life. All successful people set goals for themselves, the family, at the workplace and also for the activities in the communities where they live. Everyone needs these goals.

What happens when you have a definite goal before you? The message is immediately relayed to the mind. The mind, in turn, sets a success mechanism into action. You begin to attract information and support to achieve the goal. For example, you have a long weekend, and want to take your family for a memorable holiday. The moment you accept this holiday as a goal, you announce it to your family. You make a phone call to your travel agent. He sends you a travel brochure about the place you desire to visit. Suggestions pour in from your spouse and children. You look into the possibilities of travel by air, rail or road. You look at possible stay arrangements. You inquire about the places you must visit, or the activities you must participate in. Soon you have a wonderful plan for a memorable holiday with your family.

This principle holds good at the workplace and in the community where you live. The top business houses are using goals to motivate their staff to achieve more through better productivity. To derive the best benefit from goals, one must understand the basics of goals and goal setting. To be effective, a goal must be measurable, challenging, achievable, time-bound and shared.

If a goal is not specific or measurable, it cannot be a goal. It must be tangible and visible for everyone to see it as an achievement. If it were not challenging, it would not be a worthwhile goal. Only when you decide to achieve more than what you are presently doing, the goal would be challenging. It will then set you to a higher level of motivation. Goals must be practical and achievable. You cannot set a goal that you will build a palace for your family when you are living in a rented flat today. You could set a goal that you will build a comfortable house for your family. When goals are not achievable, they become counter-productive in that they discourage a person from setting a goal, or working to achieve it. It would not be right to have open-ended goals. They must necessarily be time-bound. Only when they are time-bound that one is motivated to put in greater effort. Finally, it is important that you must share the goals with the people who are concerned with them. This promotes teamwork and greater achievement.

It is not sufficient to simply set a goal. It must be written down. If more than one person is involved, everyone must have it written down. The details must also be noted. What is to be achieved? How it is to be achieved? Who will be responsible for what? Within what time it must be attained? When the goal details are written, you have the "bull's eye" before you. Aim and shoot!

According to need, the goals can be both long-term and short-term. This is important because some things take longer to achieve than others. Goals would necessarily be classified differently. The long-term goals would, however, be broken down to shorter terms, as annual, half-yearly and quarterly goals. These would further be broken down to monthly, weekly and daily goals. All companies and organisations work according to the goals set before them.

Goal setting should not be restricted only to the workplace. Persons who have to get ahead set personal goals, family goals, career goals, community goals and also retirement goals. Life is multifaceted, and it is important that every aspect of life must get importance.

An important aspect of goal setting is that when a person works to attain specific goals, the emphasis is always on what needs to be achieved, and not on the procedures to be followed. The goals are fixed, but not the procedures. Just as we find that when we cannot reach our destination because of a roadblock, we take an alternative route even if it is longer, and still reach our destination.

WORKING WITH GOALS

When setting goals some considerations are important. While the goals must be specific and easy to understand, they must refer to objects and actions. In being realistic, they must be in harmony with the current trends and the past achievements. It would also be important that they are not based upon related situations that can be misguiding. The ideal situation is that the new goal must be a step higher than the past achievement.

Setting deadlines can be tricky. It is natural to desire that a goal must be attained in the least possible time, but that is not practical. Every activity takes its own time. When fixing a deadline, ask yourself whether you have resources that are capable of keeping in tune with it? Also, is the deadline in harmony with what was achieved in the past in the same time? Would it help to put in additional resources? If it would, then would the exercise be cost-effective. A haphazard setting of goals can create disillusionment.

It would also be necessary to have time cushions for out-of-routine jobs. Without these, the schedule can go awry. Once the goal is defined and set with deadlines, it is best that all concerned must know them well. When the goals are achieved, reward the individuals responsible for the success.

> **Think it over...**
>
> 90% of laboratory and field studies involving specific and challenging goals led to higher performance than easy or no goals.
>
> — *Locke et al*

GOALS AT THE WORKPLACE

Although goal setting is important for every aspect of personal life, it is especially relevant at the workplace where one may need to set a variety of goals for different purposes. Some of the common goals at the workplace include:

1. **Product Goals.** These refer to the top quality products a business house may like to offer to customers.
2. **Operational Goals.** These refer to improvements in operations to increase productivity through better use of staff skills, technology and resources.
3. **Consumer Goals.** These refer to new products and services that consumers may desire.
4. **Secondary Goals.** These refer to goals that arise from current operations and may not be immediately important.

TIME FOR PLANNING

The need for goal setting leads a person to yet another aspect of the problem – the need for planning. One cannot set goals haphazardly. Nor is it practical or right to revise them frequently. That would take away the sanctity of having them. To set goals, one must understand personal strengths and shortcomings, and also needs and the circumstances. This makes it a serious exercise, which must be undertaken using the best of one's abilities and experience. Those who want to be good time managers always spend time on goal setting, and on planning to achieve them.

The next step after goal setting is to have macro and micro plans to attain the bigger and the day-to-day goals. This will require time. A good *Plan of Action* is always the basis for achieving what one has sought out for. It has been seen that as little as 20 minutes spent in planning could result in saving of several working hours every week. Even at the end of the day it would be worthwhile to spend just 5 minutes to plan out the next day. These little planning periods could lead one to the long-term goals, but that is where one begins any way. The bigger plans eventually guide a person to live a happy and comfortable life on a daily basis.

GOALS AND PRIORITIES

Once the goals are set, everyone would desire that all of them must be achieved as soon as practical. However, we cannot overlook that even amongst the many goals a person may have, there will be some that are more important than the others. It will, therefore, become necessary to sort out goals according to priorities. There are three kinds of priorities:

1. **Priorities of time.** Some things have to be done within a specified time. For example, filing of a tender, preparing a report, sending out Diwali or Christmas greeting cards.
2. **Priorities of importance.** Some things are more important than others and must be attended to accordingly. For example, preparing a sales forecast based upon last year's performance, or preparing a budget before the beginning of the year.
3. **Priorities of time and importance. Some things** are both important and time-bound. For example, filing of a Service Tax or Income Tax return, or getting the business accounts audited before filing a return. If the priorities under this heading are not attended to in time, they can take the form of Priorities of Crises. This situation can only be avoided through advance planning and timely action.

POINTS TO PONDER

- One becomes time-conscious by learning the attributes of time.
- Time management aims at being effective rather than being efficient.
- Time management is not efficiency gone mad. It is doing the right things rather than doing the things right.
- Nobody is born a good time manager. Time management must be learnt like any other skill.

- Developing the correct attitude towards time is the beginning of good time management.
- Time management has grown over the past century with the addition of newer and more sophisticated techniques and aids.
- The basis of good time management is working with the correct mix of goals and priorities.
- Although used most at the workplace, time management techniques are useful in all fields of life.

Step 3
Get to Know the Traitors

Some call them time-stealers. Others describe them as robbers. A few also call them time-thieves. A thief is one who steals another's property. A robber is one who takes away property unlawfully by force, or threat of force. Since no force is involved and there is no contravention of law, I prefer to use the word: traitor. A traitor is one who betrays the country or a cause.

The time-traitor is taking away valuable time from the lives of every person every day. This results in reduced individual and corporate productivity. It is betrayal because every person is trying to utilise the time well, but is deceived to lose valuable portions of it. The loss of time varies from one person to another, but it is estimated that on an average most people are losing almost one hour, or about 20 per cent of the time every day.

If this one-hour could be retrieved from the traitors and utilised in productive work, it could result in higher productivity, and also more peace of mind for an individual. This loss is not incurred in one big chunk, but rather in small portions in several activities that a person is deceived into thinking as important, but are just unnecessary. We need to know more about the activities and the loopholes that lead to this loss.

WRONG HABITS

The traitors can deceive you only because you may be careless. You let them do what they should not be doing. It begins with the thoughts. These thoughts become actions, and through sheer repetition the actions become habits. These may pertain to the time you spend at home, or at the workplace.

A popular habit with a large number of people is failing to plan. When you fail to plan, you plan to fail. Much time is lost when one is not sure what is to be done, how it is to be done, and when it is to be done. It is estimated that 20 to 30 minutes spent in planning can save you more than four hours every week. This can result in higher productivity and more leisure time. Through planning, it is also possible to do multi-tasking, where one can do two or more things simultaneously. We will discuss it later.

One habit that is letting down a lot of people is the inability to say "no" to people. It is human nature to ask for favours of all kinds. Some screen these immediately and decide what can be done, and what should be refused. There are many who fail to refuse and add on more liabilities on their time and effort, many times causing great frustration to self and family. If you want to keep your time under control, learn to say "no" when you cannot cope with the request.

One of the worst habits is simply called procrastination – the habit of putting off an activity for a future time. This single bad habit is causing great losses of time throughout the world. Another bad habit is that of not being able to take vital decisions. These need to be discussed in greater detail.

PROCRASTINATION

Procrastination simply means to delay, or postpone, an activity. It appears to be a harmless action, but the person who habitually procrastinates may experience a sense of guilt. Besides, it results in loss of productivity, and sometimes may create a crisis. This may also lead teammates and co-workers to feel that they have been let down. Occasional procrastination could be accepted as a part of working routine, but when it becomes habitual it can have serious effects.

Do not take procrastination lightly. It could be due to psychological or physiological disorders. These may emerge from deep anxiety, lack of self-esteem, laziness or a self-defeating mentality. The physiological disorder could arise from the role of the prefrontal cortex causing poor organisation, loss of attention and procrastination. This could also be due to a condition described as *Attention Deficit Disorder*.

Students who are studying several subjects, and need to meet deadlines, often struggle with procrastination, particularly because of lack of time management and study skills. Positive guidance can help them face the situation.

Psychologists explain that persons who procrastinate could either be the relaxed kind, who postpone the work in order to avoid stress, and find comfort in doing easier work or having fun, or are the tense type, who are unsure of their goals and are under pressure of time. Either way, procrastination gives the impression that a person is over-worked. This ultimately becomes a case of anxiety and stress.

Working with set goals and following correct time and work management techniques can help individuals to get over the habit of procrastination.

> **Think it over...**
>
> How mankind defers from day to day the best it can do, and the most beautiful things it can enjoy, without thinking that every day may be the last one, and that lost time is lost eternity!
>
> — *Max Muller*

DECISION MAKING

All the important positions include the responsibility of taking decisions about a variety of situations at the workplace. Even within the home, there is the need to take decisions. Many people fail to take decisions simply because it puts them to test. If the decision is right, it may go unnoticed, as just a responsibility correctly fulfilled. However, if the decision is wrong, it draws the immediate attention of everyone, and may also attract undue criticism. To avoid this situation, many people decide not to take a decision, and let things take their own course. This is wrong, and becomes a bad habit affecting the productivity.

Never be afraid of taking a decision. Not taking a decision is also a decision, and a bad one. Under normal circumstances, when you take a decision, there are 50 per cent chances that you are right, and 50 per cent that you may be wrong. However, when you weigh the pros and cons of a decision, the chances are that you are 60 per cent right. As you take more decisions, the added confidence will gradually increase the percentage to 70, 80 and more. All upcoming executives need to understand that decision-making is one of the most important abilities, and attracts the best emoluments. The top executives are paid extremely well because of their decision-making skills and abilities.

* * * * *

A man once sought work with a rich farmer. Winter was around the corner. The farmer thought of the need for firewood and hired him to cut the big logs into small pieces. The man was strong and apt with the axe, and in no time had a big heap ready. The next day the farmer gave him some more wood. The man had it chopped and stacked in no time.

The next day the farmer thought he had made the man work too hard for two days, and decided to give him lighter work so that he could get some rest. He led the man to a big heap of potatoes in the shed, and asked him to separate them out in three lots, big, medium and small. If some were damaged or bad, they could be put aside.

When the farmer went to see the progress of the work, which he thought would be complete by then, he was surprised to see that the man had hardly been able to sort out the lot. A little irritated, he asked, "What has taken you so long to sort out the potatoes?"

"It is taking the decisions that has taken me so long," the man said simply, "I cannot decide which potato goes to what lot."

* * * * *

PERFECTIONISM

A habit closely linked with procrastination is that of perfectionism, when a person desires only what is perfect. Not being able to attain perfection, the person keeps procrastinating. Thus time is lost and productivity suffers.

The important thing is to become an effective person, and not necessarily a perfect person. Rather than aim for perfection, learn to desire excellence, the ability to do the best in the prevalent conditions. To attain perfection, the circumstances need to be perfect also. That is not always possible. Therefore, pursue excellence and complete the assignment as an effective person. That would be good time and resource management.

THE TELEPHONE

The telephone has brought people closer all over the world. It has greatly contributed to making communication swifter and more effective. Mobile phones have made it possible for the telephone facilities to go into millions of homes at a reasonable cost, and certainly made life more comfortable.

However, this facility has taken away part of the time to talk rather than work. Since the call comes from a person who cannot know or see what you are doing, it comes as an interruption in the work, and even after the call is complete, it takes a couple of minutes before you can again return to your work. If we can add up the minutes lost over many calls during the day, we find that they make up a reasonable chunk of time lost.

We see this time-loss not only in the offices, but also in the homes. We all know of harassed housewives running between the kitchen, the telephone and perhaps the front door bell. To cut down on this running, many people have installed parallel telephone lines in the sitting room, the bedroom, the kitchen and even the bathroom. This has added to the utility of the telephone, but nonetheless the time used in speaking on the telephone is not always productive.

The mobile has only confounded this problem, encouraging the people to spend more time talking than using it for productive work. While it has helped in reaching out to people more conveniently, it has also encroached upon people's privacy and leisure time. Many business colleagues and prospects are now calling after business hours, very often causing irritation and resentment. Many get a curt response, but time is still lost in unnecessary conversation.

It is intriguing to notice several telephone instruments, besides the mobile phone, lying on the tables of managers in the office, but with the calls coming in one after the other, one wonders if that is all that is expected of the manager? No time is available for productive work, or for planning that is necessarily the responsibility of a manager. One wonders why so many managers feel frustrated, but the reason lies in the loss of their valuable time, discreetly taken away by the telephone.

We cannot do away with the telephone. In fact it is gradually rubbing in more into our everyday lives with everyone carrying a mobile phone, and trying to reach us. It has its own advantages and has promoted greater productivity through easier and swifter communication. However, we need to be aware that it can lead us to talking unnecessarily, taking away useful time. Telecommunication companies are reducing their tariffs because they know that they will make up their revenues by encouraging the customers to talk longer. They have laid out the bait. Will you bite? Or would you take control over your time and life? Here are a few common observations.

- People are speaking on the telephone more than ever before.
- Telecommunication companies are reducing their tariffs and offering newer services to encourage greater use of the phone.
- Doctors are suggesting that greater use of the mobile may be harmful for health. The microwaves could be a health hazard. Only time will tell.

Think it over...

As it is the characteristic of great wits to say much in few words, so it is of small wits to talk much and say nothing.

— *Rochefoucauld*

INTERRUPTIONS AT WORK

Interruptions at work come in all shapes and sizes. We have just discussed about the telephone and the mobile phone that may interrupt the work with a ring. Visitors at the workplace may come to make inquiries, meet you, or one of your colleagues. Whatever their purpose, they do interrupt the work, even if only for a few minutes. The person may want to meet your boss, and may be directed to you for a particular purpose.

Friends who have time at their hand may walk in just to say "hello" not realising that it is your working time, and such greetings may only delay whatever you have at hand. The friends drop into the office in good faith with a desire to create goodwill, but it would be proper to tell them that you are busy. The time belongs to you or your employer, and is certainly not meant for a social call.

It is not unusual for subordinates to walk into the office seeking guidance on a particular project or assignment. If you turn them away, it may give them reason to idle on the pretext that they are awaiting your guidance, whenever you can provide it. If you get down to helping them, it may cut a big chunk of your time from the work you might be doing at that time. Either way, your work is affected.

The boss or senior colleagues too could interrupt your work if they walk in to seek your opinion, or sometimes even to say "hello" and collect the office gossip. It is immaterial as to who interrupts your working routine. The important thing is that it affects your personal productivity. You will have to compensate for it either by staying at work overtime, or letting the productivity suffer at your cost. This can be serious from the point of good time management.

MEETINGS

Millions of meetings are called each day all over the world. Unfortunately, most of them achieve nothing. They are just a waste of time. Millions of man-hours are lost this way each day.

When 8 workers get together for a meeting that lasts 1½ hours and nothing tangible is achieved, it means that 12 man-hours have been wasted. This is the working time of two employees for a day. Add up their cost to the company and calculate the loss. If the participants have had to travel to attend the meeting, the additional travel time and costs only add up to the loss. This goes on day after day somewhere or the other all over the world.

A common reason for meetings that achieve nothing is lack of preparation for the meeting. It is important that an agenda must be circulated to all the persons attending the meeting. Everyone must be prepared with the necessary background papers. The physical arrangements for the meeting must be right, with no interruptions or disturbance. The meeting must start and end on time. Whoever is conducting the meeting must go step by step to achieve the purpose for which the meeting is called. In the event of anyone of the links being weak, the meeting fails to achieve its purpose.

One to one meetings are easy to call and conduct, as one person speaks and the other listens. Such meetings aim at assessing individual workers, delegating responsibility, or sometimes to reprimand an employee. It is important that even these meetings must be properly planned, correctly timed and is businesslike to be successful. Here are a few common things that must be remembered.

- Call a meeting only if there is no other alternative to achieve the purpose you wish to achieve.
- Fix a time and place that is convenient to all the participants.
- Have all background information ready for the meeting. If the participants need to bring in some important details tell them about it in advance.
- Begin and end the meeting on time.

- Ensure that only one person speaks at a time. Everyone must address his or her views to the person presiding the meeting.
- Do not allow the discussion to deviate from the subject of the meeting. If this happens intervene immediately to avoid wastage of time.
- If several subjects are to be discussed, allocate time to each subject according to the importance of the subject.
- Draw conclusions as soon as you find that the purpose has been achieved. Stop further discussions.
- Draw a *Plan of Action* agreeable to everyone.
- Follow the meeting with a memo or minutes giving the details of the items agreed upon.

If the meeting involves a larger audience, it may be necessary to make additional arrangements to receive the participants, to introduce them, or even to seat them according to their position. If formal introductions are to be made, or formal thanks given at the end of the meeting, then the responsibility must be assigned to persons who can fulfil it well.

We are in an age where video conferencing is done to discuss vital issues. However, we can overlook that meetings, small and big, are a part of our everyday life, and we need to ensure that they achieve the purpose for which they are called. If we fail to do so, it would only amount to loss of time.

LACK OF DELEGATION

When a person lacks confidence in co-workers and insists that everything must be done in consultation with him or her, the pressure of work and time build up very quickly. Gone are the days when the subordinates were unskilled and could handle very limited responsibilities. Workers are more educated today. They make special efforts to acquire skills and abilities. With rapid advance of Information Technology and its impact on many professional and business fields, the younger workers are well ahead of many of the managers, who failed to keep up with the rapidly changing work situations.

It is not practical to work individually. If you must succeed, you will need to work as a team. Responsibilities must be delegated to individuals. Everyone must know what is to be achieved. They must also know how and by when it must be achieved. The team leader coordinates the activities of all the members. Together they share success, and sometimes failure. When there is no teamwork, failure is certain.

We see this teamwork almost everywhere – in educational institutions, in medical institutions, in business and industrial houses and also amongst professionals, who work together to cover a wide range of activities and services.

Success can be attained only as a team. Teamwork does not mean to be an undividable group operating as one to achieve everything. This would not be practical, or possible. A team is successful when it decides to agree to achieve a particular goal or objective. The team members are free to have different views on other subjects. A team member could be a partner in other teams with different objectives.

Even within a small office every individual must know what is expected of him or her. When delegating responsibility, give clear instructions. Supervise quietly. Interfere only when it is necessary. If it is necessary for a co-worker to bring a problem to you, ask him or her that you also expect a proposed solution with it. This makes it easier to sort out the problem faster without your having to spend too much of time that could be utilised in more important activities. The purpose of delegation should be to achieve more in the same time. This would ensure good time management.

Think it over...

Time drinketh up the essence of every great and noble action, which ought to be performed, but is delayed in the execution.

— *Veeshnoo Sarma*

POOR COMMUNICATION

Good communication is the basis of an effective organisation. It includes clarity in speaking, listening and writing. The body language too communicates messages that can alter what is said or heard.

It has been observed that in every organisation more communications are sent out and received than is really necessary. A substantial portion of these can be avoided or cut down. Therefore, the next time you need to send out a communication, ask yourself: Is it necessary? Send it only if you feel convinced that it would enhance productivity.

A lot of time and effort is wasted every day when people fail to comprehend what is communicated to them. In every office a large number of letters, circulars, memos, notings and emails are circulated and exchanged. Yet human nature is such that many of these are not understood, and workers fail to carry out the instructions. Ultimately, productivity suffers.

To be effective, a communication must be clear, concise and complete. It must be addressed to the concerned persons. For a message to be clear, the person must clearly know what he or she desires to communicate. The message must be clearly worded. Many times words could be interpreted in several ways. Finally, one must ensure that the message has reached where it was sent.

To be concise the message should say just what is necessary. Many people are guilty of writing long letters or circulars. What could have been written in just 200 words is written in 500 words, taking a longer time to write, read and comprehend. The secret in making a message concise is in editing it ruthlessly after it is written for the first time.

To make the message complete, ensure that all the relevant information is included in the message, or the necessary attachments are there. This is particularly so when a meeting is called, and no agenda included in the message.

When communicating verbally, it is certainly necessary that the words are correctly chosen, and also that the body language is in harmony with the message that is being communicated. For example, you cannot reprimand a person with a broad smile on your face. You must seem as serious as the message you are communicating. In the same way, when you make a verbal presentation, you must exude the confidence by the way you stand and address the audience. Your appearance and opening remarks must attract their attention to the message you are trying to communicate. If you fail at any point, the presentation can fall flat without any impact on the audience.

To reinforce the communication skills, the advance in technology has made it possible to present photographs, slides and videos to send a message through convincingly. These methods succeed if the presentation is well planned and only that what is relevant to the subject is included. The presentation may not be well received by the audience if it is lengthy and includes extraneous matter.

Listening patiently is an important element of effective communication. The persons who come to you with problems, or proposals, eagerly look forward to your giving them a patient hearing. When you fail to do so, their expectations are betrayed. They withdraw reluctantly, but this is not without affecting the productivity. Later, corrections can be both, time consuming and expensive. This would be bad time management.

Just as important as being a good listener it is equally important to be able to read correctly and use the information to enhance productivity. If something can be interpreted in more than one ways, it is important that an immediate clarification is sought. This will ensure that you have understood whatever is being communicated to you.

Many times it is necessary to take notes during meetings and presentations. It has been noticed that on many occasions the notes may not convey something in the same spirit that the message is conveyed verbally. This could be due to differences in perception, or even the use of words in making the notes. This can be a serious setback to effective communication.

The ability to communicate effectively is not acquired automatically through formal education in schools and colleges. A deliberate effort needs to be made regularly to be able to speak, write and convey messages, and equally important, to receive those that are communicated to you in the correct spirit and word. That would add to your productive use of time.

LEISURE TIME

Leisure time is a quiet traitor. Since it comes in the garb of a pleasant break, it is always enjoyable. The few extra minutes during the tea or coffee break, a little gossip during lunchtime, or a few minutes spent every morning to say "hello" are always welcome. However, these "few" minutes cut into productive time, and add up to a lot at the end of the week, or by the end of the month.

Efficiency experts agree that small breaks help break monotony of routine, and prevent fatigue and stress from setting in. This way they help productivity. We cannot cut out this expense of time altogether, but need to be careful that here is a loophole that the time traitor is aware of. When we are careful we can cut out the wastage.

In a large industry it was noticed that the workers tended to spend extra time in the toilets. It wasn't possible for the management to restrict the time spent by the workers, but as a simple remedy the management installed lights that had an unpleasant effect and the workers cut down on the extra time spent in the toilets.

To prevent tea or coffee break from becoming a short gossip session, many offices arrange to have tea or coffee served at the worker's desk. The water cooler is also so placed that one does not waste time. Circumstances will vary from one office to another, or even from one industry to another. Individuals will have to work out methods to tackle the wastage of time in this field.

Think it over...

Like the bee, we should make our industry our amusement.

— *Goldsmith*

MISPLACED ITEMS

Nothing else takes away as much of time as do misplaced items. This is true in the home and at office. Just when you need it, you cannot find the keys to the cupboard. Even if you do, you cannot locate your favourite shirt or necktie. Socks and handkerchiefs are always difficult to locate in the clothes.

The kitchen is a small part of the home, but it is not unusual not to find the preservative the housewife may have tucked away safely. There are dozens of items that are less frequently used, but whenever one of these items is required, it takes a long time to locate it. In the same way, those fond of books find it difficult to locate a book just when they need it. Invitation cards for birthdays, weddings and other functions are received every day. Yet, many times it is difficult to locate a particular invitation when you need it.

Papers, documents and files are always a source of great harassment when they cannot be located just when you need them. The papers and documents may be tucked away in a wrong file. The file you need may be in a wrong filing cabinet, or may be resting safely in the personal drawer of another person, who may have interest in the subject. Files taken home to complete work on a holiday may be resting safely where they should not be.

Even small stationery items like a colour pencil, a rubber, scotch tape, a letter opener, or a stapler can create havoc and wastage of time when an item is not available just when you need it. In the interests of efficiency, a variety of stationery items are required on the working desk. There must be a system to keep them in place. If not, then you should be prepared to have lost time.

SYSTEMS FAILURES

Every organisation establishes systems to handle different kinds of work. Even within the home, the husband, wife and the children understand what each person needs to do, and when. Each keeps a check on the other.

When the systems are not well planned, or there is no provision to cope with extraordinary situations, we see chaos all over. It is a common feature with government and semi-government agencies where the different departments or contractors do not coordinate work with each other. For example, when the Municipal Corporation is laying out a new water pipe, one party may be digging up the road to accommodate the pipe, another may be laying the pipe, and yet another may be responsible for filling up the earth. Finally, the road repairs may be assigned to a fourth party. It is common to see the failure of the system when the road remains unfit for use for a long time, causing hardship to the common man using the road.

When the systems are not in place, it is commonplace for different departments to propose conflicting policies, creating great confusion amongst the workers. This results in a lot of wasted time and effort.

Effective work comes from handling the priorities correctly. However, this is not possible unless the systems within the organisation are well established, and responsibilities given to people who can use their authority to issue appropriate instructions. Good planning ensures an effective system of working. This way there is no loss of time or productivity.

POINTS TO PONDER

- Unknown to everyone time-traitors are always busy.
- Time-traitors succeed because we may be careless with our habits.
- Procrastination appears harmless, but makes a serious dent in the working schedule.
- Not to take decisions in time is a bad decision.
- Telephone is a useful utility, but causes a serious loss of working time.
- Interruptions at work come in all shapes and sizes.
- Most meetings are unnecessary. Make them useful when you call them.

- When you delegate, you get extra hands to work for you.
- Poor communications cause misunderstandings and lost productivity.
- Leisure time appears pleasant. Use it with care.
- Misplaced items cause the most harassment and loss of productive time.
- For smooth sailing, ensure that correct systems are adopted.

Step 4
Evaluate Your Use of Time

Once you have understood the attributes of time, about time management and also how the time-traitor is forever cheating everyone to quietly take away time, it is necessary that you must evaluate your own use of time. What we have discussed until now pertains to people in general, but we need to be more specific. You must understand how each moment of the 24 hours granted to you is utilised. You must understand how each of your days adds up to a week, and the weeks to a month, and then a year.

How do you feel about the use of your time? Most people respond by saying that they are happy the way they utilise it. They feel that they are doing their best to make productive use of their time. However, when asked if there is a possibility to put the time to better use, most people respond with mixed reactions. They desire that they could squeeze out a little more leisure time, but considering that they are already putting in their best efforts, they have doubts if it can be done. They feel that pressures are only on the increase. How would it be possible to ease them?

How do you feel about the issue? The very fact that you are holding a book on time management in your hands is evidence that you see hope in better utilisation of your time. Yes, you can achieve much more than what you are presently doing. The doubts most people entertain about better utilisation of time are because they have been conditioned to think that what they are doing is perhaps the best way of doing things. You have already seen how time behaves, and how each one of us is losing time unintentionally through the loopholes that exist in our everyday routine.

Think it over...

We should not judge of a man's merits by his great qualities, but by the use he makes of them.

– *Rochefoucauld*

YOUR DAILY ROUTINE

Through habit everyone gets to establish and live a daily routine, which we think is an ideal way of living in our circumstances. The important point is: Is that really so? Could it not be better?

Like everyone else, you have 24 hours at your disposal every day. Considering that 8 hours are spent in sleeping, though older people sleep less, you have 16 hours to use. Let us say, these 16 hours extend from 6.00 a.m. to 10 p.m. every day. These 16 hours could be further split into 32 half-hours. Now make a chart with 32 rows, and three columns. Note down the time – 6.00 a.m., 6.30 a.m., 7.00 a.m. and so on till 10.00 p.m. in the first column.

Note down your activity at a particular time in the second column. The third column is for your remarks. Write O.K. if you think the time was spent appropriately. If you think you spent more time than was right, put a minus (-) mark. Wherever you feel more time should have been spent put a plus (+) mark. You will have a chart like this:

6.00 am	Wake up, toilet, morning tea	OK
6.30 am	Make bed, shave, have bath	OK
7.00 am	Prepare breakfast, pack lunch	OK
7.30 am	Read newspaper, breakfast	OK
8.00 am	Leave for office	(-)
8.30 am	Commuting to office	(-)
9.00 am -		
1.00 pm	Office time	OK
1.00 pm	Lunch time	OK
1.30 pm –		
5.00 pm	Office time	OK
5.00 pm	Leave for home	(-)
5.30 pm	Commuting to home	(-)
6.00 pm	Have tea, rest	OK
6.30 pm	Exercise, go for walk	(+)
7.00 pm	Socialise, meet friends	(+)
7.30 pm	Help children with homework	OK
8.00 pm	Help children with homework	OK
8.30 pm	Have dinner with family, watch TV	OK
9.00 pm	Watch TV	OK
9.30 pm	Watch TV	OK
10.00 pm	Go to bed	OK

From this chart it is evident that of the 16 hours of waking time, 8 hours were spent at office with half hour for lunch. About half hour is consumed in waiting and meeting colleagues. That leaves 7 hours of working time. Whether this time is spent usefully, or not, we shall study a little later.

In the morning two hours are spent in bathing, dressing, eating and reading the newspaper, besides the few minutes spent in making the bed. One full hour is spent in commuting, because it involves walking to the bus stop, waiting for the bus, and finally reaching the office just about time, or sometimes 5 minutes earlier. The same one-hour is spent in the evening. Sometimes it takes longer because of rush. Two hours spent commuting each day is on the higher side. It is certainly tiring and time consuming. One hour could be saved if one were to go on a motorcycle instead of travelling by bus. Therefore, it is marked (-).

In the evening, half hour is spent in rest over a cup of tea. One hour is utilised for exercise, walk and socialising. One hour is spent to help the children with their homework. Half an hour is spent over dinner, and then another hour watching the TV, before ending the day at 10 p.m.

From the chart it is also evident that the hour that could be saved from commuting time is partially to be adjusted in the leisure time in the evening. It is not evident how the morning half-hour saved will be utilised, but probably it will be utilised to make the morning routine less rushed.

TIME BREAK-UP

The fore-going example of the daily routine describes a normal day. But there will be variations and pressures on this routine. There will be the need to cope with emergencies, sickness, invitations from colleagues and friends and other needs of the moment. The analysis of the time shows that whereas 8 hours are spent sleeping, another 8 hours are spent working. That leaves one with 8 hours for personal use, for the family and for social activities. These 8 hours are used for two principal activities – utility time and discretionary or leisure time.

One cannot cut excessively on utility time. The time spent in bathing, dressing and eating cannot be excessively restricted. If one were to rush through these activities, would life be worthwhile? After all, the purpose of our working is to be able to live well. It would be unfortunate if we cannot do that. The commuting time to office and back can also not be restricted for obvious reasons. Some people, particularly in the larger cities, try to squeeze some time out of sleeping time to be able to spend it on social activities. Occasionally, it might be all right. However, done on a regular basis, it affects health and personal productivity.

This leaves the discretionary time only at the disposal of an individual. During this period one needs to indulge in activities through which one derives satisfaction (hobbies, watching TV), spend time with the spouse and children and indulge in social activities.

Of the total 8 hours available for utility time and discretionary time, the balance between the two depends upon the individual's attitude towards time, and personal preferences for various activities. On an average, it is estimated that while 3 to 3½ hours are utilised as utility time, the rest is spent as discretionary time.

> **Think it over...**
>
> Well-arranged time is the surest mark of a well-arranged mind.
>
> – *Pitman*

MAJOR AND MINOR USES OF TIME

In general, the time is utilised for personal care, for the home and family, for a vocation, with friends and to interact with the society.

The major and minor divisions of time, as used for various activities, are a matter of personal need and preference. To most people, the time spent at work is a major use of time, because it is at the workplace that income is generated and one is able to make progress in life.

Some do not give importance to utility time spent on personal care and eating, but for many this is a major use of time. They give great importance to eating time, where they expect the family to co-operate and join in the activity. Shopping for food and other requirements could be a minor use to many people. To save on time, many prefer to do shopping in larger quantities once a month. Prayer time or visit to a temple, mosque or church too is a major use to many people, while some do not give it much importance.

The time spent with the family is very important to most people. Everyone desires to spend quality time with the family, supporting them in every activity, including a vacation. The attitude toward friends and social activities varies with the individual attitude. The few good friends are included in the family, and the others are given a lower priority. How individuals divide time between various activities depends upon their attitude towards time and the activities.

PRODUCTIVE AND NON-PRODUCTIVE USE OF TIME

All good time managers emphasise upon the productive use of time. What exactly does it mean to an average person? Productive use of time does not mean, "keeping busy". It refers to the time spent on activities that a person desires to accomplish. These activities are linked with goals, or targets, a person may have set. A productive activity must take one closer towards the goal. Most of these activities pertain to the workplace where the achievements are immediately visible. For example, the drawing of a building made by an architect would be a productive use of time. However, a drawing by a child may just be a recreation activity.

Watching a cricket match on the TV may give much pleasure to the family, but it would be a non-productive use of time, as the family does not accomplish anything tangible by watching the match. In the same way, window-shopping is great fun to many people, but it is a non-productive use of time, because ultimately nothing is achieved by this activity. We saw how the time traitor takes away a lot of productive time even at the workplace, causing unseen losses. Therefore, it is important that one must understand when time is being utilised for productive purposes, and when it is just being wasted away.

ATTITUDE TOWARDS TIME

Everyone looks at time differently. People grow up with time values as based upon their education, upbringing, family values and personal experiences. In general, people can be divided into two distinct categories. The first category includes people who are extremely time-conscious. You will notice that they prefer to keep their watches a few minutes ahead of the right time. They feel incomplete without a wristwatch. They have wall clocks in most of their rooms. These keep reminding them of the time. Even if they wake up at night, they look at the watch to find out what time it is. When travelling, these people prefer to carry a small alarm clock with them. These are the people who feel time is a limited commodity, and it must be correctly utilised.

The second category consists of people who feel that they have the time that they need. They wear watches, and do have fancy clocks adorning their homes, but they could not be bothered about being punctual for appointments. These are the people who reach late at parties and meetings. However, they never feel guilty about keeping other people waiting, or even about causing inconvenience to others. We see politicians invariably always reaching late for meetings. They are guided by their own feeling of self-importance, and not by time.

To which category do you belong? Perhaps you are not very sure. Some will immediately accept that time is very important to them, and they belong to the first category. Very few admit belonging to the second category, but the truth is that many people are careless about time. As a compromise, many will say that they belong to another category – a mixture of the two kinds of people we have discussed.

For people who desire to get ahead and be successful in life, good time management is very important. They are forever on the lookout to improve their personal performance and productivity. To be able to identify their own strengths and limitations in this field, it becomes necessary to carry out a self-appraisal of one's activities as related to time spent upon them. Most people are unable to do it on their own. The questionnaires that follow will be helpful.

Think it over...

There is not a single moment in life that we can afford to lose.

— *Goulburn*

SELF-APPRAISAL OF PERSONAL TIME

Earlier, we saw how an average individual spends his or her time. There are several activities necessary to live a normal life. Time is divided between them according to need and pressure. We also saw how several activities appear essential, but we spend more time than was necessary on them. This results in a lot of wasted time. Therefore, it becomes essential to look at the many activities within the home, the workplace and in the community where we spend and also lose time. To distinguish activities where an individual has control, or where one does not, the activities have been treated separately.

To carry out a realistic self-appraisal it is necessary that you should mark your response to each of the statements honestly. You can fill in the responses in privacy and need not share them with anyone. They are only for your personal use. They will help you understand your own strengths and limitations. For your convenience, all the questionnaires have been prepared in the same way, and also you need to mark them using the same basis. If your response to a statement is **never**, you should tick or circle 1. If it is **sometimes**, you should mark 2. If your response is **usually**, mark 3 and if it is **always**, mark 4.

PERSONAL WORKING HABITS

Your personal working habits influence your attitude towards the use of time more than anything else. Listed below are common everyday habits that we see everyday. Mark you responses by ticking or encircling the appropriate number.

1. I do not rush in the mornings because I like to begin the day on a positive note. 1 2 3 4
2. I skim-read the newspaper at breakfast time. I mark articles for later reading. 1 2 3 4
3. I begin the day with a list of things to be done. I prepare the list a day before at closing time. 1 2 3 4
4. I review the work-list in the morning to mark the order of priority. 1 2 3 4
5. I always work according to priorities. 1 2 3 4
6. I never put off till tomorrow what should be done today. 1 2 3 4
7. I always strive for effective work rather than for perfection. 1 2 3 4

8. I skim-read trade magazines when they arrive, marking articles for later reading. 1 2 3 4
9. I have stopped subscribing to magazines that I do not have time to read. 1 2 3 4
10. I take a decision as soon as the problem and the relevant details are before me. 1 2 3 4
11. In the event of a serious problem I try that nobody panics. 1 2 3 4
12. I always try that the problem must be resolved as soon as possible. 1 2 3 4
13. I spend a few minutes everyday to plan improvements in my working routine. 1 2 3 4
14. I never carry any work home. 1 2 3 4
15. I review my work every evening. 1 2 3 4

Add up all the numbers that you have ticked. If the total is 30, or less, you need to pay special attention to your working habits. If the total is between 31 and 45, you have good habits, but need to strengthen those habits where you have scored less. 46 and above indicates that you are in control. Manage your time to the best of your ability.

RESPONDING TO THE TELEPHONE

When Graham Bell gave telephone to the world, he could not have imagined the impact his invention would have on the way mankind thinks and works. He could also never understand that the telephone would become a sophisticated instrument, to be found not only in offices, but also in every room of the home. The modern generation cannot think of a life without telephone. At the touch of a button, it is now possible to talk to friends and relatives anywhere in the world.

Each day as the telecommunication companies push the tariffs down, people are encouraged to speak more on the telephone. Since not all conversation is productive, the telephone tends to encourage many people to waste their time. How does the telephone affect your time at home and at the workplace?

1. I have a secretary who screens all the calls.	1	2	3	4
2. If I am busy I ask my secretary to take a message.	1	2	3	4
3. I spend more time listening than talking when responding to incoming calls.	1	2	3	4
4. I try to limit all outgoing calls as far as possible.	1	2	3	4
5. If I need to provide time-consuming information, I tell the caller that I will revert back later. I do so when free.	1	2	3	4

Add up all the numbers that you have ticked. If the total is 10, or less, you need to pay special attention to your use of the telephone. If the total is between 11 and 15, you have good habits, but can strengthen those areas where you have scored less. 16 and above indicates that you are in control. Manage your time on the telephone to the best of your ability.

MOBILE PHONES

More than the conventional telephones fitted in homes and offices, the mobile phones have revolutionised life where we find everyone using these. These phones have undoubtedly increased productivity and brought people closer. However, with added facilities and !ower tariffs, people, particularly the younger generation, is going overboard. More time is being used on the mobile phones than is necessary. Are you using it to your advantage?

1. I do not give my mobile number to everyone.	1 2 3 4
2. I keep my mobile phone switched off when I can be reached on the phone at home and office.	1 2 3 4
3. I use the mobile phone only when I am away from home or office.	1 2 3 4
4. When driving, I always stop the vehicle before responding to a call.	1 2 3 4
5. As far as practical, I limit my calls on the mobile.	1 2 3 4

Add up all the numbers that you have ticked. If the total is 10, or less, you need to pay special attention to your use of the mobile phone. If the total is between 11 and 15, you have good habits, but can strengthen those areas where you have scored less. 16 and above indicates that you are in control. Manage your speaking time to the best of your ability.

INTERRUPTIONS

People lose more time because of interruptions than for any other cause. What are your experiences in this field?

1. I do not encourage my friends to call on me at office.	1 2 3 4
2. I have a fixed time when my subordinates meet me for consultation and reporting.	1 2 3 4

3. I have a fixed time for visitors to call on me by appointment. 1 2 3 4
4. My assistant has the lists of people who can interrupt me, and those who can do so only in special circumstances. 1 2 3 4
5. I close my office door when I am in the midst of planning a project. 1 2 3 4

Add up all the numbers that you have ticked. If the total is 10, or less, you need to be careful about the time lost because of interruptions. If the total is between 11 and 15, you are aware of the problem, but can strengthen those areas where you have scored less. 16 and above indicates that you are in control. Manage your working time to the best of your ability.

MISPLACED ITEMS

Just like interruptions, misplaced items at home and at the workplace result in a lot of wasted time and effort. To counter this problem one needs to be personally disciplined, and also that everyone in the office must follow established systems. How do you fare in this field?

1. I rarely misplace my keys. 1 2 3 4
2. I have a fixed place for all the stationery items that I use. 1 2 3 4
3. I always keep an extra pencil and ball pen in my working desk. 1 2 3 4
4. On every document I mark the name of the file where it must be filed. 1 2 3 4
5. We use files of different colours for every department. 1 2 3 4

6. Before closing for the day, I ensure that all the files must be returned to the appropriate filing cabinets. 1 2 3 4
7. I review the filing cabinets periodically to ensure that the files are placed properly. 1 2 3 4
8. I clear my table of all loose papers before I leave office every evening. 1 2 3 4
9. I clear up the drawers in my working desk once every month. 1 2 3 4
10. Our office observes good housekeeping norms. 1 2 3 4

Add up all the numbers that you have ticked. If the total is 20, or less, you need to be careful about misplaced items. If the total is between 21 and 30, you are aware of the problem, but can strengthen those areas where you have scored less. 31 and above indicates that you are in control. Manage your working time to the best of your ability.

DELEGATION

Four hands can do more work than two hands. Ten hands can do even more. To succeed in the modern world, it is necessary that work must be shared with others. The trend is towards working as a team, rather than as individuals. To add to one's productivity, it is essential that part of the work must be delegated to others. They learn to handle greater responsibility, and you become more productive. How do you fare in this field?

1. In our office we work as a team. 1 2 3 4
2. Everyone in the office knows what is expected of him or her. 1 2 3 4

3. In the office we are like an extended family, which share both the difficult and happy moments together. 1 2 3 4

   1 2 3 4

4. I delegate responsibilities because that ensures the training and growth of all employees and productivity. 1 2 3 4

5. When a subordinate brings a problem to me, he or she also brings a possible solution 1 2 3 4

6. I always keep in touch with all my staff. 1 2 3 4

7. I always follow up on delegated work.

8. I encourage my subordinates to put in their best performance. 1 2 3 4

9. If a subordinate makes a mistake, I always call him or her to my cabin to talk. 1 2 3 4

10. I convey gratitude heartily to those who perform well, or do something exceptional. 1 2 3 4

Add up all the numbers that you have ticked. If you score 20 or less, you must delegate responsibilities more than what you are doing presently. If the total is between 21 and 30, you are aware of the problem, but can strengthen those areas where you have scored less. 31 and above indicates that you are in control. Manage your working time to the best of your ability.

COMMUNICATIONS

In any home or office there are a variety of communications, both incoming and outgoing. The purpose of all communications is to enhance productivity, but if they are not effective, the time is just lost. How do you rate your communication skills?

INCOMING COMMUNICATIONS

1. I skim-read a communication as soon as I receive it. 1 2 3 4
2. I read the communication in detail later. 1 2 3 4
3. I have asked my assistant to present all the mail at one time.
4. I mark the important portions in the mail and forward it to the appropriate person with my remarks. 1 2 3 4
5. If a letter needs my personal attention, I put it aside and respond to it before leaving office. 1 2 3 4
6. I read a Fax message as soon as I receive it, and mark it to the appropriate person for response. 1 2 3 4
7. I read the mail received through courier along with the other mail before lunch. 1 2 3 4
8. I read the mail received through courier in the afternoon at 4.00 p.m. every day. 1 2 3 4
9. I encourage my subordinates to write short memos and reports only. 1 2 3 4
10. I make sure that the In-tray does not get overloaded. 1 2 3 4

Add up all the numbers that you have ticked. If the total is 20 or less, you need to handle the incoming communications with greater care than what you are doing presently. If the total is between 21 and 30, you are aware of the problem, but can strengthen those areas where you have scored less. 31 and above indicates that you are in control. Manage your incoming communications to the best of your ability.

OUTGOING COMMUNICATIONS

1. I send out a memo only when it is very necessary. 1 2 3 4
2. If a message can be sent and confirmed through email, I do not send a letter. 1 2 3 4
3. When writing a memo / letter, I make sure that it is clear, concise and complete. 1 2 3 4
4. For convenience I have standard letters typed out on my computer. 1 2 3 4
5. I personally read and check all my outgoing mail. 1 2 3 4

Add up all the numbers that you have ticked. If the total is 10 or less, you need to give more attention to outgoing communications than what you are doing presently. If the total is between 11 and 15, you are aware of the problem, but can strengthen those areas where you have scored less. 16 and above indicates that you are in control. Manage your outgoing communications to the best of your ability.

MEETINGS

More time is wasted in meetings than most people imagine. Many meetings fail to achieve what they are expected to. Therefore, one must review how meeting time is utilised. How do you fare in this field?

1. I call a meeting only when it is necessary. 1 2 3 4
2. I ensure that the meeting agenda reaches the participants in time. 1 2 3 4
3. I always reach the meetings in time.

4. I always carry the complete background material to the meeting. 1 2 3 4
5. I ensure that the meeting starts on time. 1 2 3 4
6. I ensure that all the participants get an opportunity to speak.
7. I do not get angry if any of the participants disagree with me. 1 2 3 4
8. I always keep an eye on the clock. 1 2 3 4
9. I always try that the meeting must achieve the purpose it is called for. 1 2 3 4
10. I always end a meeting on time. 1 2 3 4

Add up all the numbers that you have ticked. If the total is 20 or less, you need to be more careful how you handle meetings presently. If the total is between 21 and 30, you are aware of the problem, but can strengthen those areas where you have scored less. 31 and above indicates that you are in control. Manage your meetings to the best of your ability.

USE OF COMPUTER

Unfortunately, those who joined their vocations a decade ago, or earlier, are handicapped in not having been exposed to computers. The younger lot has an edge in being able to handle computers easily. We cannot overlook that computers have changed the way people think and work. Computers have added to effectiveness in every field of work. Their use is only growing. How do you rate yourself on computers?

1. I try to upgrade my computer skills regularly. 1 2 3 4
2. I am able to use word processing and spreadsheet software on my computer. 1 2 3 4
3. I have the software for storing vital data, my appointments and priorities. 1 2 3 4
4. I follow a definite system to create and maintain folders and files. 1 2 3 4
5. I feel that use of computers has added to efficiency in my work. 1 2 3 4

Add up all the numbers that you have ticked. If the total is 10 or less, you need to give more attention to your computer skills. If the total is between 11 and 15, you are aware of the problem, but can strengthen those areas where you have scored less. 16 and above indicates that you are in control. Manage your use of computers to the best of your ability.

EMAIL MESSAGES

It has become commonplace to communicate through email. It is swifter and effective, if both the sender and the recipient open their mailboxes everyday. Besides it is very cost effective. Email has opened the world to everyone, making international communications swift and easy. How does email affect your functioning every day?

1. I read my email at a fixed time each day. 1 2 3 4
2. I respond to the mail immediately after reading it, or forward it, if necessary. 1 2 3 4

3. I keep the email on my computer for some time in case I need to refer to it later. 1 2 3 4
4. I delete unnecessary email immediately on receiving them. 1 2 3 4
5. I clear up my computer of all old mail every three months. 1 2 3 4

Add up all the numbers that you have ticked. If the total is 10 or less, you need to give more attention to your use of email. If the total is between 11 and 15, you are aware of the problem, but can strengthen those areas where you have scored less. 16 and above indicates that you are in control. Continue to use email to add to your effectiveness.

FAMILY TIME

It does not matter what you do. The time spent with the family is as important as the time spent at work. A person's vocation is intended to help a person live well with the family, and not to keep away from the family. Those who live a balanced life ensure that enough time is allocated to spend quality time with the family. How would you rate yourself on this score?

1. I make it a point to spend the evenings with the family. 1 2 3 4
2. The family always eats dinner together. 1 2 3 4
3. I always help the children with their homework and studies. 1 2 3 4
4. I meet my friends and socialise when I go for the evening walk 1 2 3 4
5. I spend one day every month exclusively with my spouse. 1 2 3 4

Add up all the numbers that you have ticked. If the total is 10 or less, you need to give more attention to spending time with the family. If the total is between 11 and 15, you are aware of the problem, but can strengthen those areas where you have scored less. 16 and above indicates that you are in control. Ensure that the family never has reason to your not spending quality time at home.

LEISURE TIME

Just as important as time with the family, the friends, and at the workplace is the time you spend on personal leisure. Do remember that it is your life. You should not let your everyday activities rob you of your time. Leisure activities not only help recharge the system, but also protect one from boredom, anxiety and stress. It also helps promote creativity. Do you have any leisure time in your time schedule?

1.	I watch the TV with my family every evening for one to two hours.	1	2	3	4
2.	I reserve one hour every week for my hobbies.	1	2	3	4
3.	I read at least one book every month.	1	2	3	4
4.	I take two short vacations every year instead of one long vacation.	1	2	3	4
5.	I plan my vacations ahead of time by making travel arrangements, hotel reservations and other plans in advance.	1	2	3	4

Add up all the numbers that you have ticked. If the total is 10 or less, you need to give more attention to personal leisure. If the total is between 11 and 15, you are aware of the problem, but can strengthen those areas where you have scored less 16 and above indicates that you are in control. Plan your routine to have enough leisure time.

PLANNING TIME

Very few people allocate time to this important aspect of time management. It is important to plan every aspect of your life, and follow the plan in your everyday life. It will ensure you success in every field. How would you rate yourself for your planning activities?

1. I have set long-term goals for the next five years.	1	2	3	4
2. I have broken the five-year goals into one-year goals.	1	2	3	4
3. I always break up the one-year goals into quarterly and monthly goals.	1	2	3	4
4. I break up the monthly goals into weekly and daily goals.	1	2	3	4
5. Everyday I prioritise the tasks I have at hand.	1	2	3	4

Add up all the numbers that you have ticked. If the total is 10 or less, you need to give more attention to your planning activities. If the total is between 11 and 15, you are aware of the problem, but can strengthen those areas where you have scored less. 16 and above indicates that you are in control. Never compromise your time on planning activities.

YOUR STRENGTHS AND WEAKNESSES

As you look back at the scores of different aspects of your life, you will begin to appreciate the areas of your strength, and also where you need to improve your activities. At this stage, you should make a list of both your strengths and weaknesses. In the next step we will look into the factors that may be holding you back.

> **Think it over...**
>
> There can be no persevering industry without a deep sense of the value of time.
>
> — *Lydia H. Sigourney*

POINTS TO PONDER

- To become a good time manager, one must periodically evaluate the use of personal time.
- Your habits, good and bad, dictate the daily routine.
- Outside pressures like emergencies, sickness, invitations from colleagues and similar interruptions create pressures on one's everyday routine life.
- Individual needs and preferences differentiate between the major and minor uses of time.
- To be a good time manager one must be able to differentiate between productive and non-productive activities and use of time.
- Personal attitude towards life and time influence an individual's use of time.
- A person must be aware of activities over which one has control and also those that beyond normal control.
- Good working habits lead to productivity at the workplace.

- The telephone has promoted productivity, but is also the cause of a lot of wasted time.
- Items that are misplaced and the interruptions at work can both be a big waste of time.
- Sharing work through delegation increases personal productivity.
- Good communication skills are useful both at the workplace and in the society.
- One must watch out for unnecessary and badly organised meetings.
- Computers have revolutionised the way people think and work. Use them to your advantage.
- Family and leisure time are just as important as the time spent at the workplace.
- A good time manager is aware of personal strengths and weaknesses.

Step 5
Learn to Change Yourself

After you have appraised how you have been spending your time in the past, it becomes necessary for you to understand what activities add to your effectiveness, and also what activities are just activities, and do not help achieve anything. In being a good time manager, it is not necessary to be busy, or to fill your time with activities. The important thing is to be involved in activities that make you effective. What is ultimately necessary is to develop skills and abilities that help you achieve more in less time, or help you produce the same thing with lesser effort. It is equally important that you must enjoy a satisfying life. To be able to do this, you will need to understand yourself better.

WHY ARE YOU WHAT YOU ARE?

Have you ever realised that you are a unique person? There never was one like you before you came to this world, nor is there one like you today, and there will never be one like you in the future. You were born unique, with qualities from your parents and forefathers. As a unique person, when your inherent qualities react with the circumstances and the environment that surrounds you, the unique characteristics are further strengthened. It is the combination of the many unique characteristics in you that make you what you are – a very special person!

With every individual being unique, does it mean that people have nothing in common with each other? No. Being unique only means that every individual reacts differently to given circumstances. Otherwise, the traits of human beings are similar. God has given everyone the choice to accept whatever one likes, and reject what one does not like. It is this choice that makes some people capable and effective, and the others just live ordinary lives. You are also free to choose whatever kind of life you wish to live. You may experience some constraints, because of what you have learnt from your parents, your teachers and your friends and relatives, but then you have chosen these influences and constraints of your own choice. Nature, or God, do not in any way compel you to choose one way of life, or another.

How do your choices help shape your life? This is possible because of your actions based upon your choices. With repeated actions one develops habits, and individuals are often distinguished because of their habits, good or bad.

> **Think it over...**
>
> Every organisation of today has to build into its very structure the *management of change.*
>
> — *Peter F. Drucker*

HABITS – THE BUILDING BLOCKS

You are known by the kind of habits that you have. When good habits predominate, one is known as a good person. In the same way, when bad habits are conspicuous, a person is obviously avoided. Good habits are important to individuals who want to get ahead in life. Like other habits, the ability to manage one's time well, or otherwise, is also a habit. Therefore, a person's immediate concern is to develop the habit of utilising the time to the best of one's ability. Some learn this at a very young age in school; others just overlook it or prefer to do whatever they find easy and pleasant. Many people are averse to the discipline necessary to be a good time manager.

Habits are not formed overnight. They are the result of repeated actions day after day. With each repeated action, an activity gets ingrained into the human subconscious to become a habit. Every habit has its foundation in a thought. Through this thought, one visualises what one wishes to do. The visuals motivate one to action. When actions are repeated, it becomes a habit.

As a little child, one picks up food items with the hand and puts them into the mouth, messing up both the hands and the area around the mouth. At that stage, any efforts to ask the child to eat with a spoon fail. However, gradually, by watching everyone else eat with a spoon, the child learns to eat neatly. If taught, the child will not only learn how to use a spoon, but also learns how to use a fork and knife effortlessly. The Chinese teach their children to eat with two chopsticks held in the same hand, manipulating them effortlessly to eat slippery noodles, and also rice and vegetables. A habit gets so deeply ingrained into the subconscious that even if it were dark, or a person is blindfolded, one would still take the spoon to the mouth.

Eating with a spoon is just one example. Bathing, wearing clothes, eating and drinking, riding a bicycle or scooter, driving a car or another vehicle, writing on paper or the blackboard, doing a variety of things in the office, and even in a factory, are all a part of us as habits. We do all these activities without the least effort. Through sheer repetition every day actions have become habits.

The habit of good time management is taught early in school, when every child is expected to reach at a fixed time. The classes are for a fixed time. The teachers spread out the curriculum over a fixed period. Every child is expected to complete each class in one year. With such adherence to discipline of time, followed up by a similar regimen in college and at the workplace, is it not unfortunate that one slips into carelessness and loses control over time? Learning good time management can be as easy as going back to your school and college days, and inculcate the same discipline into your adult life.

Think it over...

Regret for time wasted can become a power for good in the time that remains. And the time that remains is time enough, if we will only stop the waste and the idle, useless regretting.

— *Arthur Brisbane*

POSITIVE AND NEGATIVE CONDITIONING

One single factor that holds back the vast majority from adopting good habits is negative conditioning. If we were to carefully look at the society in which we live, we would be shocked to find that 19 out of every 20 persons are negative oriented. When such a large number is in the grip of negative thinking, is it surprising that people fall an easy prey to negative actions?

This world is inhabited by two kinds of people. The vast majority looks at each other for mutual acceptance and admiration. This is often referred to as "keeping up with the Joneses". It is for this reason that people buy things they have no use for, build huge houses that they cannot maintain, and spend lavishly on weddings and other occasions to "show off" that they are no less than others. Many of these activities make them uneasy and unhappy, but they indulge in them saying, "Whatever will others think of us?"

There is a smaller minority that does what is in harmony with their conscience. They could not be bothered what others think of them. They have their own beliefs and convictions, and follow their own mind. The difference between the two groups is that while one is conditioned by the negative influences of the vast majority, the smaller group stands firm, following the voice of their own conscience.

To which of these two groups do you belong? The choice is yours. It is for you to choose whether you would like to face the criticism of the vast majority, or just fall in line with the community. It is only one out of 20 who stands up like a leader, follows his or her own convictions, and proves that that is the right path to follow.

Just as with other activities, this holds good to individual perceptions of the utilisation of time. Not bothered by the vast majority we find people who are punctual, and put the time to best use to get ahead in life and also enjoy personal fulfilment and happiness.

Think it over...

Observe a method in the distribution of your time. Every hour will then know its proper employment, and no time will be lost. Idleness will be shut out at every avenue, and with her, that numerous body of vices, that make up her train.

— *George Horne*

MAKING A BEGINNING

When you decide to turn a new leaf in your life, and become a good time manager, it is a positive step on your part to improve yourself. We must remember that a journey of a thousand miles begins with a single step. This first step has to be a positive attitude towards time. Look at it as a valuable resource, a gift from God. Despite all the follies all of us commit everyday, every morning God grants each one of us another day to live a complete life. Look at the day as a beautiful day, full of the finest opportunities for you to grow and find fulfilment.

The next step to remember is that you are what you think you are. If you think you are ineffective, you are inviting failure. Acquire abilities to get ahead in life. Believe in yourself. Keep reminding yourself that you can do it. When things go wrong, as sometimes they will, use the mistakes as building of personal experience. After all, experience is what people learn by making mistakes. You, too, can add to your experience and grow.

A good balanced life is possible only when a person is possessed of a variety of skills and abilities. What should a person do if one is lacking in some of these? There is only one way to handle this situation, and that is to acquire the skills that are lacking in you. Never be shy of learning. There are people who keep learning new things all the time. The best thing is that despite frail health people can still grow mentally. To become a good time manager, you will need to:

- Live a balanced life where you have time for your family, at the workplace, for the society, and for personal leisure and growth.
- Protect yourself from physical and psychological burnout that can be caused when you are unable to cope up with the pressures of some aspects of everyday life.

STEPPING TOWARDS SUCCESS

To achieve early success in attaining your objective of becoming a good time manager, remember that it is all in your mind. Success must begin from your thoughts. You will do well to follow these simple guidelines.

- Always think of success, and not failure.
- Let everyone know that you are learning to be a good time manager. Once you make your intentions public, others will remind you when you go wrong.
- Believe in yourself. You can do it if you really want to. Remind yourself of your own skills and abilities.
- Remember that negative thinking is a destructive habit. It takes the same amount of effort to think positively as it does to do negative thinking.
- Never make negative comments about yourself. Many do it to seek sympathy. You cannot rise this way. You have to do it through personal effort.

- Counter negative suggestions with positive statements. With a vast majority in the grip of negative thinking, you are bound to get your share of negative suggestions. Be prepared to counter them unhesitatingly.
- Set definite time management targets for yourself. We have discussed this earlier. Make plans to achieve these targets. Follow up with action.
- Build your confidence slowly by attaining what you set out to do. Smaller successes will lead you to bigger successes, gradually building your confidence.
- Deliberately make an effort to get over your shortcomings through proper assessment, understanding the causes and correct planning and execution.

GETTING OVER LIMITATIONS

It is natural to want to get over one's limitations to be able to get ahead. Earlier, you assessed yourself on the basis of certain parameters, and checked your scores. You might have scored well in some activities, and not too well in others. If you have been honest with yourself, the scores would have guided you to your own strengths and weaknesses. Let us revise the activities and work out ways to have a balanced approach towards every aspect of life.

Personal Working Habits

Let us get back to the self-appraisal chart on personal working habits. The chart serves two definite purposes. First, it is a guide that lets you know your strengths and weaknesses in this field of activity. Second, you get to know that if you adopt all the activities, you would have good working habits. But it is not enough only to know what is right or wrong. The important thing is how to make it a part of life. Some of the facts that emerge from this self-appraisal are:

- Begin the day on a positive note.
- One should not waste much time on the newspaper.
- Advance planning is important.
- It is necessary to work according to priorities.
- In setting priorities aim for effectiveness, and not perfection.
- Procrastination must be avoided.
- Time should not be wasted on unproductive activities.
- Decisions must be taken when necessary.
- Problems should not create panic. They must be faced calmly.
- At the end of the day, the work must be reviewed and a plan made for the next day.
- Work and family life must not be mixed.

Some of these activities appear very simple and easy to adopt. However, the truth is that they require a consistent effort before they can become habits. We will revert to these later.

Telephone and the Mobile Phone

The next two self-appraisal charts pertain to use of telephones and the mobile phones. Again, you will notice that some important facts emerge from these two questionnaires.

- The use of telephones and mobile phones impose heavily on efficient utilisation of time.
- If one is not time-conscious, there can be great wastage of time speaking on the phone.
- Most people tend to speak excessively on phone. The situation must be handled without causing offence.
- One must learn to speak as little as possible to communicate through phone.

> **Think it over...**
>
> Don't let the telephone control your life; use it to enhance the purpose of your life.
>
> — *Anon*

Interruptions

In the next self-appraisal chart you might have noticed that much time is lost because of interruptions. Once again, important facts emerge from this questionnaire.

- Most visitors do not realise that the person they call upon may not be free to talk or attend to them.
- Few people realise that calling on a person without an appointment is really an interruption on the person's time. He could be busy with some important assignment.
- We do not have a direct control on people who come calling without an appointment.
- It is an important problem that needs very tactful handling. Lack of tact can cause loss of goodwill.

> **Think it over...**
>
> You cannot stop all of them who interrupt you, but you can stop most of them.
>
> — *Anon*

Misplaced Items

Misplaced items at home and at the workplace result in a lot of wasted time. It is common to blame others for this lapse, but in reality one is personally to be blamed for this situation. The self-appraisal chart will help you pinpoint your own weaknesses. The basic reason for this problem is the lack of a system, or systems covering various aspects of one's life. Some important facts emerge from this questionnaire.

- Misplaced keys cause more time loss than other things.
- Unavailability of a pen or pencil when you need it urgently is another irritant.
- Misplaced documents, letters and other papers are known to create havoc in the workplace.
- Clear filing instructions, files of different colours and designated places for each set of files helps counter loss of time and effort.
- The adoption of definite systems helps locate whatever you need.

Delegation

The false notion that others may not do a job as well as you prevents many from delegating a part of the responsibilities to others. This is known to affect the productivity of people. The self-appraisal form can help tell you of your strengths and weaknesses in this field. You will do well to re-enforce your strengths, and plan out special efforts to get over your weaknesses. Some facts emerge from this questionnaire also.

- Teams work better than individuals.
- The team members must be clear on what are the goals, and what is expected of each member of the team.
- Cordial relationships enhance productivity at the workplace.
- Delegation helps people grow. Just as the subordinates grow in their skills and abilities, you too grow with them.
- Follow up of responsibilities delegated to others is necessary.
- Mistakes must be tactfully explained, and good work must always be appreciated and rewarded.

Communications

Communications, both incoming and outgoing, are an important part of everyday workplace activities. They would obviously consume valuable time. The important thing is that not all communications are important. Some are urgent, others important and some are only of routine nature. All need appropriate attention. Some facts emerge from the questionnaire.

- One needs to differentiate between different kinds of communications – urgent, important and routine.

- Proper handling of communications helps save time and effort.
- It helps when the communications are clear, concise and complete.
- One must send out brief communications and encourage others to do the same.
- There must be a definite system to handle communications at all levels.
- To be effective, communications must be appropriately supervised.

Meetings

Millions of meetings are organised each day around the world. The most unfortunate truth is that these meetings waste millions of man-hours of those who participate in these meetings. This has a detrimental effect upon individual productivity. You will need to be conscious about it. Here are a few facts that have emerged from the questionnaire.

- All meetings are not necessary.
- Many meetings fail because of poor planning.
- Few people are able to keep control over the meeting time.
- All participants in the meetings must know what is expected of them.
- Those who can handle meetings well enhance productivity at all levels.

Computers

Computers have invaded every aspect of life, making life easier, but also difficult in the sense that now one needs to be computer literate. The younger generation is doing it at school level, but for those who have been working for more than a decade, has had to add on this skill to be competitive. The questionnaire has brought out certain facts.

- A computer is the nicest thing to happen to revolutionize life at all levels.
- It is important to upgrade personal computer skills regularly.
- A computer is not a display piece on the office desk. It is a great efficiency tool.
- One needs to experiment how personal efficiency can be enhanced through use of a computer.

Communications have been revolutionised through use of email. Every office is using it to enhance productivity. You too can do it. However, do not let your life rotate around emails. You will do well to note the facts that emerge from the self-appraisal questionnaire.

- Emails have revolutionised the way people communicate.
- This form of communication has opened the doors to a lot of useless communications, often wasting one's time.
- Like other activities, one needs a definite system to handle emails.

The Family

The need to live well personally and offer the best care to the family motivates people to work harder. However, it is common for people to forget this and get involved in their work more than is necessary. Many times even the personal needs are overlooked. This is not the right situation. It can lead to serious problems. Time with the family and leisure time must get the importance they deserve. Some important facts emerge from these two self-appraisal questionnaires.

- The family is the very purpose why people put in hard work.
- Ignoring the family can give rise to problems that are not easy to resolve.
- It is everyone's duty to help and guide the children to become useful citizens.
- Building good friendships help fill the vacant moments of life.
- The leisure time helps persons to relax and avoid stress and tension.
- A holiday is as important as work.
- One must be involved in self-development activities.

> **Think it over...**
>
> Punctuality is a compliment you pay the intelligent and a rebuke you administer to the stupid.
>
> — *W. Somerset Maugam*

Planning

Finally, you cannot afford to ignore the time that must be spent on planning. This is the most important aspect of time management. How have you fared in this self-appraisal questionnaire? Observe the facts that emerge from this questionnaire.

- Planning means to know your destination. Unless you know it, you cannot reach there.
- Planning means setting long-term and short-term goals, to be further broken into annual, quarterly, monthly, weekly and daily goals.
- Planning means to work to priorities. You will need to differentiate between what is urgent, important and just routine.
- Time spent in planning is recovered manifold through great savings of time and effort.

GETTING TO ACT

You have just gone through a variety of facts and observations about different aspects of your life. Review them once again. Do it a little differently this time. Mark each statement with either a 'S' or a 'W'. If you feel that the statement describes a point of strength in your life, mark it 'S'. If you consider it a personal weakness, mark it 'W'. Now you have a list of both your strengths and weaknesses. Note them down separately on paper. While you would like to re-enforce your strengths, it is also time to get over your weaknesses.

For each weakness, write what you can possibly do to get over it. Also note by when you can do it. This can be said to be setting a small goal. To achieve this goal, you will need to make a *Plan of Action.* This way, you will have a series of small goals that you want to attain, and also a series of *Plans of Action.* Can any of these be combined? If so, do the needful. From amongst the list of goals, mark ones that are more important than the others. You might like to number them 1, 2, 3 and onwards, number 1 representing the most important one. Allocate time to achieve all the goals, one by one over a set period.

A common fault by most people is that they keep these goals in their mind as activities they wish to undertake. This is not right. To be effective, the goals must be listed on paper. The *Plan of Action* too must be worked out on paper for you to see, work on and sometimes review and redesign. Soon you will find that you are well on your way to become a good time manager.

PLAN OF ACTION

Several issues will come before you as you review the self-appraisal tests, and plan action on each one of them, combining some and acting on others independently, a grand plan will emerge before you. This is a plan you need to execute to develop habits that can become a part of the day-to-day life, taking you towards more successful living. To ensure that the *Plan of Action* is balanced, you will do well to check the following:

- Will the plan help you to become a more effective person?
- Does the plan have time for you to live comfortably?
- Does the plan include activities and time for the family? For the spouse? And the children?
- Will you be more effective at the workplace?
- Does the plan have time for social activities? For the friends? For community service?
- Does the plan provide for leisure activities? For your hobbies and extra-curricular interests?
- Will the plan provide you time to unwind, de-stress, and relax?

- Does the plan provide time for planning activities on daily, weekly and long-term basis?
- Does the plan provide a timeframe to achieve whatever is desired?

Once you know that there is a provision for everything, you can be sure that it is a balanced plan, and you will benefit by it. Take special note of the timeframe and deadlines. Now you have a roadmap to becoming a good time manager.

THE KEYWORD

Action is the keyword to attaining what you have set out to. Go back to the earlier part describing how habits are formed. They begin with a thought. The thought is: I want to utilise my time well. I want to become a good time manager. Why? I want it because it will make me more effective at home, at the workplace and in the society. It will ultimately make me a better person. How? This will be possible through a positive well-balanced *Plan of Action* that is before me.

Plans are only plans unless they are executed. To execute the plan, you will need to act; you will need to do what you have not been doing earlier. It will not be easy because it will require deliberate action that you are not used to. If you are convinced of the cause and committed to it, it will become easier. With each repeated activity, it will become simpler, because it will pass on from the conscious mind to the subconscious, and gradually become a habit.

Remind yourself of your school days, and the discipline that is part of the school life. You did it for a long time. You carried it partially to your college life. Why did you let it slip by for the sake of personal choice? When you bring the discipline back to everyday life, it will not only become easy, as it would have become a habit, but it will also add to your personal effectiveness.

PLANNING TO SUCCEED

Of all the habits that contribute to managing time well, the habit of planning all the activities is most important. No amount of emphasis on this issue is enough. To simplify the issue it is good to remember that good time managers:

- Spend a few minutes at the close of the day to plan for the next day.
- Spend about 20 minutes on the last day of the week to plan for the next week.
- Set both long-term and short terms goals broken into annual, quarterly and weekly goals.
- Review the activities periodically.

Deanna Mascle has suggested that everyone must remember time management by expanding the four alphabets used to spell T – I – M – E.

T – Take time to plan.

I – Involve others to help you.

M – Meditate and reflect on your goals and dreams.

E – Evaluate your priorities and goals.

Think it over...

The hours of a wise man are lengthened by his ideas, as those of a fool are by his passions. The time of the one is long, because he does not know what to do with it; so is that of the other, because he distinguishes every moment of it with useful or amusing thoughts; or in other words, because the one is always wishing it away and the other always enjoying it.

— *Addison*

POINTS TO PONDER

- You are a unique person. There never was one like you before you, nor there ever will be.
- You are known by your habits – good and bad.
- The negative conditionings by the people we are surrounded by hold us back from becoming more productive.
- You have great potential within you. Develop your latent skills and abilities.
- When you think success, you will attain success.
- Personal limitations hold back people from growing. It is equally true that limitations can always be overcome.
- To be effective, develop positive personal working habits.
- Do not let the telephone steal your valuable time.
- Make it public that when you are at work, you do not like to be interrupted.

- Unless you develop a system, you will continue to lose time because of misplaced items at home and at the workplace.
- Teams achieve more than individuals working independently.
- A good communicator is always appreciated.
- Improved computer skills enhance personal productivity.
- The family is the very purpose of all your efforts. Do not ignore to give your time and effort to it.
- Planning at every level of life leads one to great success.
- Learn to recognise and differentiate between your strengths and weaknesses.
- Develop a *Plan of Action* that covers all aspects of life.
- Action is the keyword to attain whatever you desire in life.
- The habit of planning will lead you to perpetual success.

Step 6
Efficiency Aids and Techniques

Mankind has forever been trying to find ways to make the work less burdensome and yet more effective. The primitive man shifted from scratching the soil with sticks to using a wooden plough. The wooden plough was later replaced with steel ploughs, tillers and a variety of other implements to make the procedure for growing food and other necessities easier. The digging was initially done by hand. To increase efficiency, it became common to use animals like bullocks, horses and camels. Further improvisations were done when a variety of tractors and equipment were devised to work swiftly and effectively.

The use of new techniques was not restricted to agriculture only. Mankind has continued to establish industrial units to fulfil human needs. Even within the industries, there is a continuous search for more productive methods and procedures. In almost every undertaking the workers are challenged to find out ways that would reduce effort and cost, and at the same time increase productivity. Workers who propose improved techniques are rewarded through salary increments, promotions and recognitions through awards.

This only goes to show that mankind has always been trying to find out better ways of doing things. However, they did not call it better time management, which it really was. Few linked productivity and time. Better ways of doing things and use of efficiency aids improved productivity, and really meant better utilisation of time in everyday life. It touches every aspect of life. Mankind has devised efficiency aids to make life more comfortable and productive. The process has only gained momentum with time.

> **Think it over...**
>
> Both optimists and pessimists contribute to our society. The optimist invents the aeroplane and the pessimist the parachute.
>
> — *Gil Stern*

EFFICIENCY AIDS IN THE HOME

The basic purpose of all human activity is to find comfort and happiness oneself, and for the family. You may not be aware of it, but an average home is loaded with efficiency aids that make life more comfortable.

When mankind did not find the atmosphere within the home comfortable, when it was too cold, or two hot, fireplaces were built to heat the homes to make life comfortable. Gas and electric heaters replaced the fireplaces. Today the market is flooded with a variety of heaters to fulfil all kinds of needs to suit whatever an individual can afford. To combat the heat in summers, a variety of coolers were devised. Window air conditioners, split air conditioners and central cooling have further added to personal comfort. Mankind is forever trying to find the ultimate in personal comfort, but the end is not in sight.

The furniture in the home is so designed to fulfil different kinds of needs and provide the level of comfort desired. The placing of the furniture is also so done as to permit easy movement within the home.

The common call bell used in almost every home has undergone a lot of improvement over the years. A variety of chimes beckon the householders to the door. Used as an efficiency aid, the use of the call bell can tell you whether it is the milkman, the vegetable vendor, the housemaid or the children returning from school. Cordless call bells help call the domestic help.

The human need to keep in touch introduced the telephone to homes. At one time, there would be one phone that everyone used. Now we see telephones in every room of the house. The busy people insist upon having them even in the bathroom and the kitchen. Small exchanges installed within the homes make it possible to talk from one room to another.

A small slip pad may seem too elementary to be called an efficiency aid, but ask a person who needs to note down a telephone number or a message. Those who seek efficiency keep slip pads with a pencil or ball pen near every telephone instrument, and also in the kitchen to note down items, which need to be replenished. This way a purchase list is ready when you go to the market.

In many homes, the slip pad near the telephone in the living area is supplemented with a small white board or display board where social engagements, wedding invitations and other appointments are noted. Another popular place for a white board is the kitchen where items that need to be replenished are noted on the board instead of on a slip.

Another efficiency aid in the home is a calendar with large digits. It is not only used as a conventional calendar, but also simultaneously serves the purpose of recording the milk received from the dairy, the newspaper and magazines received. This way, at the end of the month, it is easy to tally the supplies received.

Efficiency experts have not overlooked the bathrooms in the homes. They are no longer what they used to be. In the present times, even the bathrooms are turning hi-tech. We do not just have hot and cold water available, but also a variety of taps and showers for personal comfort. The variety in washbasins, bathtubs, water closets and bidets is no less. People indulge themselves to relax and be comfortable, as they take their daily bath, a part of their utility time.

We cannot overlook the need for wall clocks in the home. All time-conscious people have clocks in key areas like the living room, the dining area and the formal living area. It is common to have a timepiece on the bedside table. This would normally have alarm facilities. Watches and clocks always surround people who are very eager about putting their time to best use.

Think it over...

There is scarcely any less bother in the running of a family than in that of an entire state. And domestic business is no less importunate for being less important.

— *Montaigne*

KITCHEN AREA

The kitchens too are now hi-tech. Great effort is made to design kitchens so that all the available space is utilised. Accessibility to the storage area is important. Besides the shelf top working space, the areas of activity include the stove, the wash area and the refrigerator. Depending upon the space available, a kitchen can be designed in many ways. In each design, care is taken that the least amount of movement is necessary between the three work areas. An important aid is a chimney over the gas stove. An exhaust fan too is essential. A ceiling fan is best avoided.

Have you noticed how many efficiency aids can be seen in any kitchen today? Initially most kitchens had two gas stoves. Today, the kitchen tops are with four stoves. This is to enable the cook to handle many things at the same time. The refrigerators now come with icemakers, deep freezers and compartments to store vegetables and fruits. Even the storage boxes come in a variety of shapes and sizes to fully utilise refrigerator space.

The market today offers equipment that can blend, mix, extract juice, grind and do a whole lot of other things to ease the efforts of cooking. Besides these, there are a variety of toasters, grillers, ovens, sandwich makers, pressure cookers, steamers, and gannets. Ice cream makers, and what not? Each day there are new additions to efficiency aids in the kitchen.

One may think that a knife is a knife, and having one in the kitchen would fulfil the needs for cutting vegetables in the kitchen. No. The modern kitchen has a variety of knives used for many kinds of activities in the kitchen. To mention a few, there are knives for paring, for cutting vegetables, for slicing bread, for carving meats and a whole lot of fine knives for decorative cutting of vegetables and fruits.

The ingenuity of man has provided eating spoons in several sizes – soupspoons, tablespoons, dessertspoons and teaspoons. A less popular variant is the coffee spoon used with small coffee cups. Forks and knives also come in different sizes for different purposes.

Cookware too has changed with the times. From the conventional copper and brass cookware, there is a shift to nonstick cookware, ready to serve cookware and cookware that can be used in ovens and microwaves.

Increasingly, in many homes, both the husband and wife are working. This leaves lesser time and energy for cooking. Therefore, it is natural for enterprising people to come forth with new equipment and ideas to make cooking swifter and requiring lesser effort. You can appreciate how people are learning to use time better, often compensating it with additional equipment and efficiency aids in the home. This trend will continue in the future.

Kitchen Efficiency Tips

With lesser time available to the housewife, here are a few time-tested tips for an efficient kitchen.

- The workplace must always be clean and free of obstacles. The top surfaces and walls must be easy to clean.

- There must be a distance of 5 to 7 feet between the three areas of functioning – that is, the stove, the wash area and the refrigerator.

- Do not have the cooking stove in front of the window. It can be a cause of accidents.
- Always have the dish rack above the wash area. The water will drip into the washbasin.
- Provide pull-put storage for easy accessibility and cleaning the storage area. It is not the amount of storage space provided, but it's placing that is important for efficiency in the kitchen. Do not have any storage area above the stove.
- Keep electricity points away from the wet area.
- There must be ample lighting in the kitchen.

THE DUSTBIN

Few people may have looked at it that way, but the dustbin is one of the most useful efficiency aids ever designed by mankind. It serves a useful purpose both at home and in the office. In many homes, we see little bins even in the bedrooms or dressing rooms to dispose wads of cleansing cotton or tissues, or in bathrooms. The kitchen always has a large bin because there is much for disposal by way of vegetable peels, waste paper, leftover food, etc. The kitchen bins are best lined with a plastic bag for easy disposal and cleaning.

The dustbin plays an equally important part in the office. Every office table needs one. The only way to keep the paperwork in order is to follow the simple rule: Dispose it or dump it. Either respond to it yourself, or pass it to another person for response. If it is not necessary, dump it. The wastepaper bin is the place for it. If you want to be effective, periodically review the papers you may have tucked in your working desk. Dispose them or dump them.

Whenever you look at the dustbin, look at as a great efficiency tool. Use it to be effective.

A DIARY

A diary is perhaps one of the earliest efficiency aids devised by people, who are conscious about the need for being effective. In all likelihood, a diary has emerged from the common notebook used to keep records. A diary is really a combination of the notebook and the calendar. Diaries come in all sizes and shapes. Diaries provide a lot of common data useful in everyday life.

There are many specialized diaries, like the ones used by lawyers, who note down the details of the cases listed on a particular date. There are others used by engineers, the medical profession, tax specialists and others. The specialized diaries list a lot of data that is relevant to a particular profession.

The most popular kind of diaries has one page for a day. The page could be blank, but mostly it is ruled for writing conveniently. The diaries used by businessmen may have rows mentioning time of the day to record appointments. Almost all diaries have a page for recording personal information, and may also have pages to record important information like renewal of licences, payment of insurance premium and other similar information.

A table diary with one page to a day is most popular to record all kinds of information pertaining to a particular day. One may record things like total sales made, money collected, the number of clients or customers met. It may also list appointments for the day, important things that need attention, or important communications or phone calls to be made. At the end of the day it would be a list of things that needed to be done, and what has been achieved. If something needs to be carried forward, transferring the information to the appropriate page could do it.

With the diary as the principal record of activities for the day, the information could be transferred to appropriate heads and places as required, or fixed as a part of the daily routine.

TELEPHONE AND ADDRESS BOOK

A telephone and address book is yet another very popular efficiency aid used by all effective people. Standard address books of various sizes are available in the market. These have pages marked by alphabets so that names can be recorded alpha wise. Many have place for the name and address on the left side, with separate columns to record the office and residential telephone numbers. Many have provision to record the fax and the mobile numbers also.

Most people prefer to maintain two address books, one for the office, where the names and addresses of business colleagues are recorded, and the second one for the home, where names and addresses of relatives and friends are recorded. While one is useful in the office, the other is used at home. The one for the home must also list the telephone numbers of the children's school or college, the family doctor, the nearby nursing home, the police station, the railway station and bus terminus numbers, and details of local theatres, restaurants and hotels. If you avail of home service offered by grocers, the electrician, plumber and others, their telephone numbers must also be on the book.

The telephone numbers keep changing. Therefore, it is necessary that depending upon need, the address books must be revised periodically to ensure that the numbers are relevant and correct. Since many people now own computers and have an Internet id, this may also be recorded in the records, even though the information could be stored directly on the computer.

VISITING CARD HOLDER

Most businessmen and service personnel carry visiting cards giving their credentials, business address and telephone numbers. Many prefer to hold these cards in a card holding album. This is very much like a photo album, but the plastic jackets have smaller pockets to hold visiting cards. These are more popular in the office rather than at homes, and could be a useful efficiency aid. Visiting card holders come in a variety of sizes to suit individual need.

BUSINESS PLANNERS

A business planner is a combination of a diary and personal record. A variety of business planners are available in the market. Depending upon the size, the quality of paper and the variety of information that can be recorded, some of them can be said to be expensive. A planner is essentially different from a diary is that it may not only include a diary of a smaller size, as compared to the conventional one day to a page diary, but there will be greater emphasis on personal record of a lasting nature, with sections for projects and plans, record of customers, personal travelling, accounts and a whole lot of other information.

A telephone directory may also be a part of the planner. A planner may have a section on favourite quotes and prayers that inspire and motivate. In contrast to a diary, a planner is in the form of a leather bound file, and the diary part and other sheets can easily be replaced in the following year. Of course these will have to be purchased from the same vendor.

A planner may be designed at home for personal needs on a spiral notebook with a lasting cover, and divided into sections as required. It may not have a conventional diary, but a calendar could be included, and information recorded as and when necessary. One could customize the planner to fulfil personal needs.

Most of the professionally produced planners are good, but bulky and unwieldy. They cannot be easily carried about. Despite these disadvantages, planners are popular with the business community and sell in large numbers. The upper crust of businessmen has moved from keeping a diary to using a planner. Those not involved in much planning activity can opt for small table models that can be placed on the worktable like a tent card.

> **Think it over...**
>
> It is more than probable that the average man could, with no injury to his health, increase his efficiency fifty percent.
>
> — *Walter Dill Scott*

DIGITAL DIARIES

With everything getting hi-tech, the conventional diary too has taken a new form in the form of a digital diary. It can be conveniently carried in the coat pocket, or in the brief case. Operated with cells, the digital diary can be used to maintain a database of addresses, telephone numbers and important memos. It can also be used as a calculator.

The price of a digital diary depends upon its storage capacity and the additional facilities available. Like all other equipment, these diaries need to be kept away from dust, heat and moisture. It is also important that when replacing cells, great care should be taken otherwise the stored data can be lost. At one time, these diaries had become very popular, but with the coming of the mobile phones, their popularity has come down.

CALCULATORS

At one time, many of the serious-minded individuals were sceptical about using calculators lest they lose their ability of making fast calculations, when maintaining office records and accounts. However, it was not long before they realised their mistake, and took to using calculators.

A calculator has become one of the most effective time saving productivity tools for innumerable applications. With many businesses providing door-to-door service to retail stores and homes, a calculator is useful to draw out invoices quickly and accurately. Almost every businessman who needs to make calculations keeps a calculator on his worktable. Models of the size of a powder compact come especially for housewives so that they can make quick calculations when shopping.

Most calculators are capable of making complicated calculations. Considering the more specialised kind of calculations required in different businesses and professions there are special models for scientific calculations, financial calculations of interest, and for a variety of other needs. Cells or solar energy can power calculators. Everybody needs one.

TELEPHONE DIRECTORY AND YELLOW PAGES

Every home and office needs a telephone directory to access numbers that are not required everyday. The directory supplied by the Telephone Department to every subscriber suits the purpose. The important numbers must be noted on the first page of the directory. The directory is often bulky, and people tend to place it away. It must be available conveniently.

In the larger cities, a directory of selected services, popularly known as Yellow Pages is available. It provides a lot of useful information in general, and about the business and professional activities in the town. A copy can be obtained from the publishers, or a good bookseller in the town.

EFFICIENCY IN THE OFFICE

An office is a place for business and professional activity. It is important that all the activities there must be directed towards attaining greater productivity. Since at this stage we are discussing only the efficiency aids, we will restrict to the subject of office equipment only, and consider the organisational aspects later.

At one time, there was not much to discuss about office equipment, because besides the office furniture and the telephone, the only other equipment were typewriters.

Incoming and outgoing mail formed an important part of office routine, and this involved writing letters, getting them signed and packed. There was also much promotional literature that needed to be mailed. Addressing and sticking postage stamps was important and time consuming. One of the earliest equipment that entered the larger offices was a Franking Machine that did away with buying and sticking stamps on letters, packets or parcels. In the recent times, keeping in view the time consumed in communication through post, most business organisations have started using courier services. They pick up mail from the office, deliver it in the least possible time, and also tender proof of delivery. The competition amongst courier companies has made it an effective service at a reasonable price.

Teleprinters were employed in some offices to speed up the communications. With better telephone services and facsimile machines, it became possible to send letters and documents in their original form, and soon teleprinter services were eliminated. People took to using handy fax machines that could be connected to a phone anywhere.

Initially, for better communication, offices had an internal inter-com system for talking within the office, and the conventional telephone was used for talking outside the office. However, with the introduction of smaller EPBAX models, one can use the same handset to talk within the office, or outside. When the office is closed, an answering machine enables the callers to leave messages. Communication has indeed become very swift.

The conventional typewriter was not being ignored either. Some of the offices moved on to electric typewriters, but electronic typewriters that had the capability of storing documents to obtain additional copies of the same document soon replaced these. The quality of printing of these typewriters compared with printed documents. The letters produced on these machines put forward an enhanced image of the organisation from where these documents originated.

The use of electronic typewriters too was short-lived, because it had become possible to reduce the cost of computers and printers. In the beginning, the computers were fairly elementary, but their capacity to store documents and information, and the ability to correct and produce correct documents made them an attractive choice. The printing was done on dot-matrix printers because of cost considerations. It was not long before inkjet and laser printers began to replace the dot-matrix printers for everyday use. The documents produced were of better quality than those produced on electronic typewriters, and were cheaper. Offices were fast getting hi-tech.

Computers and accessories were getting better and cheaper. Even those who thought computers were not for them were surveying the markets how they could derive benefits from them.

The last decade (1996-2005) has brought about a revolution in the office, the factory and the home. Computers have changed the way people think, work or communicate. What took months earlier can now be done in minutes. Computers have linked the whole world like one big office. Even within the office, the computers are networked, and different software is available to everyone. Accounting in the offices is done totally on computers. One can monitor figures every week, or even on a daily basis. Performing results are announced to the shareholders every three months. Nothing could be more satisfying.

Computers are no longer restricted to the office table. Laptops at very reasonable prices have made it possible for executives to work even when they are travelling, or when they are compelled to remain at home. Executives keep in touch with their offices even when they are on vacation. Attached to a phone or a mobile set, it keeps them updated wherever they are. The smaller models are handheld. It is difficult to assess where we are heading.

Depending upon the need, a variety of printers are available at reasonable prices. Few people are using dot-matrix printers for specific assignments. The smaller firms are using inkjet and the small laser printers, but the bigger companies have installed high-speed network laser printers, which print swiftly. Combination equipment where the facilities of a scanner, printer and fax are available is very popular now. Colour laser printers too are within the budgets of most companies. Equipment is now readily available at reasonable prices.

The Photostat machine is yet another piece of equipment that has changed the communication scene everywhere. These machines are required in almost every area of life, and standalone Photostat Centres have provided employment to many people, but their use in government offices where a large number of copies are required to be made and provided everyday, has added effectiveness to this activity.

As can be appreciated from what has been discussed, the modern office has a big variety of equipment that requires skilled workers to operate and get the best out of them. The office is no longer a place where papers and files moved from one desk to another, but is a technical operation where everyone works like a team.

> **Think it over...**
>
> We used to have lots of questions to which there were no answers. Now with the computer there are lots of answers to which we haven't thought up the questions.
>
> — *Peter Ustinov*

BAR CODES

The use of bar codes is yet another efficiency procedure to enhance productivity and save time. A bar code was initially a series of parallel lines and bars of varying width with spaces printed on a surface, but have further evolved into patterns of dots, concentric circles, and hidden within images. These are further being developed into matrix codes in the form of a grid of square cells, referred to as 2D barcodes. Stacked barcodes are an intermediate form of 2D barcodes and linear codes, formed by traditional linear symbols placed in an envelope that allows multiple rows. The width and spacing of the bars and other graphics represent binary information that can be read by an optical scanner connected to the computer.

Bar codes have made it simple for swifter billing of products in supermarkets and department stores, doing away with the problem of tampering with price labels by the customers or the staff. These also make it possible to monitor stocks. Bar codes are equally important as a document management tool. Airlines are using bar codes to track passenger luggage, just as car rental companies use them to track their cars. Nuclear waste is also being tracked with bar codes. Some fashion designers are using these codes to identify outfits to be displayed by different models. These are equally useful in marking books, and for use in libraries. Each day their use is on the increase.

Although first patented in U.S.A. in 1952, bar codes did not catch the fancy of users until the 1980s. Since the popularity of bar codes is comparatively of recent origin, manufacturers are gradually beginning to use them. One can expect far-reaching enhancement in productivity through use of bar codes.

MOBILE PHONES

The improvement in telephone services and the use of fax and Internet services made communication swifter and more effective. Like the computer, in the past decade, the introduction of the mobile phones has revolutionised the way people work. It is now possible to keep in touch with each other at all times. Their great popularity has enabled the services to become cheap, and reach the most distant corners of the country.

A mobile phone is not only a communication tool, but is equally popular as a mobile music system, and in many cases as a camera also. Every few months, we see new models with more facilities, and probably lower price tags.

Companies are using mobiles not only to keep in touch with their personnel at the international or national level, but equally so locally, where even the smaller organisations are using these to direct and guide their sales and service staff. Even the good things have their shortcomings. Mobile phones have encouraged the younger generation to talk more, thus affecting loss of productive time. The secret in controlling the situation lies in teaching everyone to speak only as much as is necessary.

DISPLAY BOARDS

It is not unusual to see display boards in offices, displaying some of the products and services the company deals in. All service-oriented businesses now have white display boards where service calls are immediately noted. A white board marker and a rubbing pad are kept available near the board. The list of the calls enables a person to handle calls in a particular locality in one visit. Different people handle separate areas. This way unnecessary travel time is saved, and at the same time better service is provided to the customers.

These boards are also used to list service assignments, and the time by when they will be completed, and the equipment returned to customers. This way it is possible for the customers to get the information without having to ask anyone for the details. One is able to see such boards at the railway stations where the late arrival or departure of trains is noted. This makes the work easy for the person sitting at the enquiry window. These boards are also used outside examination halls, in hotels and restaurants and in a whole lot of ways to provide information without having to waste time and manpower on it.

The electronic version of these display boards is to be seen at airports where the arrivals and departures of different flights are displayed.

USEFUL KITS

Although a ball pen may be the most important thing to work in an office, there are several other items necessary for effective work. The most popular pen colour is blue-black, or a darker version of blue, one needs to have one each of green, red and black pens also to mark documents in certain circumstances. A black felt pen is useful to mark files and packets. Besides these, one needs a pencil, sharpener, rubber and scale. A letter opener or paper cutter, a pair of scissors, stapler and pins, clips and cellotape is useful. If filing is done, then a punching machine is a must. A stamp pad and some binding thread would complete a kit on an office table.

Just as these items make a good office kit, people keep first aid kits in the office, home and even in a car. It would also be useful to keep a kit of a variety of tools at home for minor repair work. Those who are fond of household handiwork keep larger kits. Another useful kit maintained by many ladies is a sewing kit with a pair of scissors, a variety of needles and threads and the most commonly used buttons for ready repairs at home. In the same way, people who travel much keep a ready travel kit that has all the essentials one uses everyday. Those who need medical care keep medical kits. Most women keep a tube of burns ointment in the kitchen.

The purpose of highlighting the use of these kits is to become aware how people eliminate time wasters from their lives, and make available the smaller things that are required in emergent moments that come unannounced to disturb a person's time schedule.

Think it over...

If you do what you have always done, you will get what you have always got.

— *Anon*

POINTS TO PONDER

- Mankind has forever been trying to find ways to make work less burdensome.
- Every home is full of gadgets and equipment that aim at making life easy and more comfortable.
- Kitchens have now become hi-tech with a variety of gadgets of everyday use.
- Good practices help housewives save effort in a kitchen
- A diary continues to be a basic efficiency aid for everyday use.
- No home can do without a telephone and address book.
- People in business and commerce prefer to use handy planners that come in a variety of forms and sizes.
- Digital diaries are the hi-tech version of the conventional diaries.
- It is difficult to think of life without calculators available for different professions.
- Offices are now hi-tech with a variety of machines and equipment.

- Bar codes are an innovative way of marking sale prices and tracking items.
- Mobile phones have brought people closer all over the world.
- A variety of kits containing small things help make life easier in many ways.

Step 7
Living Effectively

A person is not recognised as successful only on the basis of a good career. To be truly successful, a person must live a balanced life, with time for oneself, for the family, for work, and for the society that has given in abundance to everyone. Therefore, no plan of living is complete unless it includes time and activities for all the elements that contribute to success. There must be time for personal care and growth, for unhurried meals, for leisure, for work and for relaxation and sleep. If some of these essentials were missed out, one would soon suffer a burnout.

In the management of time, you are your best friend, and also your worst enemy. The choice is yours. There is no such thing as "your time", "the employer's time" or "the family's time". It is all your time. It is for you to decide how you wish to use it. Time is not something out there, an object distinct from us. Time is a part of our lives. We need to understand it. Understanding time is to know how we are living our lives. Good time management begins with you. It relates to everything that is of interest to you.

* * * * *

Your Questions Answered...

What is the difference between investing time and spending time?

You invest time when you utilise it for productive activities. You spend it when no useful purpose is achieved.

How would you classify the time used as utility time? Is it just routine, or could it be called productive time?

It would be productive time when you use to strengthen your personal support systems. If not, then it is just routine spent time.

Is the purpose of discretionary time just to relax and avoid stress?

No. Besides promoting relaxation and physical and emotional health, discretionary time can be used to develop stronger ties within the family, amongst friends and also in the society. It can also be used to enhance personal skills and abilities. It can be used to enhance creativity and productivity.

* * * * *

MAKING MISTAKES

There is no end to the mistakes one makes in utilising time. This is simply for the reason that irrespective of all the mistakes one makes, each morning, God blesses everyone with yet another day to do as one pleases. It is for you to utilise it well, or squander it. God has given you a free choice. It is the intelligent person who learns from the past mistakes. They are opportunities in disguise. Use these opportunities to learn a better way of doing things. After Edison had failed to make the incandescent lamp even after 2,000 trials, people laughed at the great waste of time, but Edison simply said, "I have found 2,000 ways that do not work." Learning from his own mistakes, he did finally give the world a lamp no one can do without today. That is learning from time gone by. Time will not return. But one can learn from what has gone by. One who does not learn from the mistakes can only be termed a fool.

PLANNING IS THE KEY

Planning is the key to becoming effective. This has been repeated at every step. No amount of emphasis on the need for planning is enough. Those who fail to plan, really plan to fail. Unfortunately, most people hate to plan in advance. They feel that the time spent on planning is just a waste. But that is not true.

It takes only one percent of one's time to plan ahead. If one were to spend just 20 minutes, one could plan for the whole week ahead. Is that too much to expect? These 20 minutes could make the next week both comfortable and worthwhile. At the same time, as a bonus, you will save as much as up to 4½ hours each week to put to better use. If you add these over the year, you will appreciate the extra number of working days you have. Calculate it in terms of money, and you are a sure winner.

Planning will essentially mean that you adopt the following steps:

- Make a list of everything you need to do. This would be in the form of goals or objectives you have set for yourself and need to attain. They must cover all the aspects of everyday life.

- The next step would be to prioritise the list on the basis of what you have learnt about prioritizing urgent and important activities. Mark 1 for the most urgent and important activity, and move onwards to activities of lesser urgency and importance.
- Split the list to smaller lists for each activity. For instance, you could have one list pertaining to your utility time, another for time with the family, and one for the workplace. This is necessary because the nature of activities would be different, and would require a different kind of treatment.
- Can you reduce the pressure on your time by delegating some of the activities with the family members, co-workers and friends? When you seek support, you reduce some of your own less important work, and can then use that time on activities that promote greater productivity.
- Set a time frame for each activity. There will obviously be daily goals, weekly goals and monthly goals. These will together carry you forward towards annual and long-term goals.
- Prepare plans to attain goals. These plans must be in harmony with your personality. You must have the skills and abilities to follow up with the activities. When you are dependent upon others, you must have good communication skills and ability to work together as a team.
- Have a system of periodic evaluation in place. No plan is foolproof that it should not be reviewed periodically. This way, if things go wrong sometimes, you can always think of alternative ways to attain the goals.

> **Think it over...**
>
> If a man takes no thought about what is distant, he will find sorrow near at hand.
>
> — *Confucius*

HANDLING CRISES

A common every day rule is: If anything can go wrong, it will. When things go wrong, it means problems. When planning, it is necessary to anticipate problems and how they will be handled. But it is not always possible to forecast the nature or the magnitude of problems, and also when they will raise their ugly head. A problem will obviously require urgent attention, many times upsetting the normal schedule as planned.

More frequent problems occur at lower levels because there is greater action there. Therefore, the staff at the lower levels needs to handle them swiftly. This is a source of working experience to them. The problems at middle and upper levels are more complex, and need the attention of senior managers.

Problems are best handled when they begin to emerge. As they grow older, they become complex and difficult to control. Unfortunately, everyone is not able to recognise problems soon enough because of lack of knowledge and experience. To be able to recognise problems, look at the variance in what you expect and what you have. If there is a variance higher than normal, there is a problem. Get down to set it right. Remember that to set a problem right you will need to take decisions. If you don't then it is procrastination, a time traitor.

HANDLING TIME TRAITORS

It is not enough only to know that hidden all over there are traitors waiting to take your time away. They are forever trying to lure and catch you off-guard. They come in strange forms, and at odd times. You will need to be at guard all the time until it becomes a habit with you. Some of the common occasions when you can expect them to attack include the time when you:

- Get complacent and stop advance planning
- Give in to procrastination
- Cannot make a timely decision about an activity
- Go overboard with your social activities
- Decide to do everything yourself
- Fail to exercise control over established systems
- Fail to communicate effectively
- Lose effective control over your meetings
- Fail to prioritise your work.

To ensure that the time traitors do not harm you, or your plans, you will do well to:

- Periodically review if all the time-traitors are under control. If not, then identify them. Assess the loss they are causing you.
- Prepare a *Plan of Action* to control the waste of time.
- Execute the *Plan of Action* to achieve your goal.

KNOW YOUR BIORHYTHM PATTERN

Through self-appraisal exercises you have learnt about your strengths and weaknesses, as related to utilisation of time. However, a very important aspect of life is the biological variations in plants and animals, briefly discussed earlier. It is important that every individual must understand how these biological variations, or biorhythms, as they are called, affect personal productivity.

The variations in the biorhythms affecting human beings are based on the changes in the 24-hour day. These affect the body temperature, blood pressure, the level of energy, attentiveness, appetite, sleeping and waking patterns and a whole lot of activities within individuals. The moods also follow a set rhythm. The heart too beats to a rhythm. The menstrual cycle in women, and the sex drive in both men and women are also controlled by these rhythms. These can be traced to the activities of the hypothalamus and the pituitary glands. The hormones secreted by these glands are responsible for these variations. However, the details are still not fully understood. The study has given rise to the science of chronobiology.

The sleeping and waking patterns are easily disturbed when a person travels swiftly in a jet plane into areas with different timings and sleeping and waking patterns. The biological changes are described as 'jet lag'. It takes some time before the body gets adjusted to the new environments and timings. In these circumstances one should be prepared in advance by changing sleeping and eating patterns. Avoid broad daylight. Remaining within the house helps one to get over the situation soon.

It is common knowledge that an individual's body temperature is the lowest between 4.00 and 6.00 a.m. It rises gradually by mid-morning, when one feels a higher level of energy. Those who follow different sleeping patterns like sleeping late and also rising late, experience the rise in energy levels later in afternoon. No two people have identical biorhythms. Therefore, one needs to personally assess levels of energy at different times of the day.

It is now an established fact that there is a definite relationship between time and biorhythms in individuals. As the biorhythms vary at different times of the day they affect personal efficiency. At certain times individuals perform more efficiently than at other times. Taking advantage of this fact, the more difficult and challenging assignments can be handled when the efficiency is at a peak, and the routine jobs can be handled at other times. This ensures high productivity and good time management.

REPETITIVE WORK

Doing repetitive work reduces productivity. It has been observed that repetitive work produces monotony and boredom. Both of these can affect productivity. If not checked, it can lead to fatigue and stress. This can be observed in a simple thing like driving a car. Normally, everyone likes driving a car, particularly when you are on a cross-country run. However, if the journey is long, and one drives uninterrupted over a couple of hours, one notices that the concentration on the road begins to suffer. Physically also one feels cramped. Under such circumstances, it is usual for the car driver to stop for a few minutes, walk about a little to help blood circulation, and have a cup of tea or coffee, and then continue with the journey.

A similar thing happens when one is working in an office or a factory. Similar observations have been made for people working continuously on computers, or working in call centres. The repetitive work produces monotony and boredom. The best solution to counter this problem is to alternate different kinds of work while making a work plan. For instance, after a period of planning or working with documents, a person could have a break to catch on the pending telephone calls. The variety helps keep the productivity high. People have used this fact to promote productivity. Many people mix indoor and outdoor responsibilities to counter the problem, and also maintain high productivity.

MULTI-TASKING

On a computer, you could do several things together. While the music is playing gently to soothe your mind, you could simultaneously be busy writing a report on the word processing software, and also making entries into the accounting software, as the vouchers reach your table. That is putting the time to best use, doing several things without getting bored, or feeling over-worked.

Earlier, the kitchens had two stoves to enable two things to be done at one time. Now we have stoves with four burners so that housewives can simultaneously be cooking four things at a time. She could probably also have something going in the oven also at the same time. This is again putting the time and equipment to best use.

A person who is conscious of the best utilisation of time can also spread out work to increase personal productivity. There are managers who work in the office, but take a round of the factory to supervise the production work going on and at the same time to break the monotony of the work in the office. It is obvious that working responsibilities and circumstances vary from place to another. However, one can learn much from these persons and increase personal productivity. Individuals with good working skills succeed the best.

TAKING ON COMMITMENTS

Busy people attract more work. The effective worker attracts still more work. It is often said that if you want to accomplish something, seek the support of a busy person. It is natural. This might be fine from the point of view of the person who desires to get something done, but it may not be so from the point of view of the person who is asked to take on more work. The additional work means more commitments and responsibilities. It also means greater pressure on a person's time. If it is not right to be burdened with additional responsibilities, why do people not refuse it? This is simply because people find it difficult to say "no".

The next time you are given additional work, before you say "yes" to it, consider whether you can handle it comfortably. If you cannot, do not hesitate to say "no". If the other person is insistent, which many people are, set forth an alternative suggestion that would it be all right if the time limit is removed from the proposed assignment. This way, you have not said "no", but at the same time, you have expressed that you are already short of time. If the person still wants you to do it, you know that the assignment has an open-ended timeframe, and you will not be under pressure.

How does one handle the boss, who regularly passes on work to you because of your productive abilities? Under such circumstances, it is not possible to say "no", nor is it possible to ask the boss to ignore the timeframe because you are expected to understand the importance and urgency of the assignment. Think about it. If the assignment will take you upwards in your work because of the experience you will gain, or the gain of self-esteem that follows accomplishment, you may find it worthwhile to accept the responsibility. However, if you feel that the work is being piled on to you disproportionately, as compared to your colleagues, you can always respond by suggesting that a part of your routine work, or partially completed assignment, be passed on to another person so that you can put your heart and soul into the proposed assignment. Your boss will have to reconsider the priorities. This means that you have not said "no", and yet not taken on commitments that could place greater pressure on your time.

MAINTAIN INFORMATION BANK

We are living in an age when all kinds of information keep coming to us. Much of it is not useful immediately. However, there is always a feeling that some of the information may be required at a later date. In that case, it becomes necessary to store the information in a practical form for future use. This seems a logical approach to the issue, but unfortunately, the quantity of the information may be so high that the storage may offer practical problems. It may require space, and it should be so kept that it can be retrieved quickly.

It is for an individual to assess personal need for the information, and to adopt a system that works. It might be worthwhile to keep on record the source of the information. If required at a later stage, it could be requested for again. Another way is to follow a definite system to review the information periodically, and to weed out whatever appears unnecessary.

The computer has made it possible to store a lot of information without use of paper or space. Information that comes through the computer could be directly stored in appropriate dockets and files. Since a lot of information is available on websites, it might be worthwhile to keep a record of these, and follow up whenever particular information is required. Despite large disk space on the computers, information can pile up swiftly. It is therefore necessary that the records be reviewed, and all that is unnecessary is deleted to free space.

In maintaining the information bank, the effective time manager keeps an eye on the kind of information that would increase personal and corporate productivity. It is not worthwhile if it does not attain this purpose.

WORKING TO PRIORITIES

Nobody can claim that there is no pending work to be done. Even the most effective person cannot make such a claim. We have earlier seen why it is important to differentiate between what is urgent, important or routine. We have also seen how different combinations of work situations seek our attention. The secret lies in working to priorities. Every individual needs to understand what activity is both urgent and important, or whether it is important, but not urgent, or it is urgent only, but not important. The bulk of them are routine activities of low importance and urgency.

Remember the Pareto Time Principle. It simply states that if you do 20 percent of the top priority tasks, 80 percent of your work will be achieved. This means that of the ten activities we have on our daily work list, there are two activities that can carry us through to 80 percent achievement for the day. When you do more than 20 percent, the level of achievement rises proportionately. This makes it easier to quickly enhance our productivity.

It sounds too easy to be true. There must be some catch somewhere. Where could that be? The catch that you suspect about is within you. The success that comes from the use of the Pareto Time Principle depends upon your ability to prioritise correctly. When you have ten activities before you, you have to decide which two amongst them are most important, and will contribute towards your productivity. This may not be easily achieved in the beginning, but as you practice the Pareto Principle, you will soon begin to understand how to prioritise your activities.

Earlier, we have also discussed the ABC Analysis, whereby activities and situations are graded according to their importance in particular situations. You must understand how it is practised in everyday life. It will hone your skills on prioritising your activities to enhance your productivity.

Think it over...

Time exists because there is activity...Time is the product of changing realities, beings, existences.

— *Nicholas Berdyaev*

UNDERSTANDING PRIORITIES

The simple way to fix priorities, as discussed earlier, could be to describe them as urgent, important, or routine. But how does one truly understand the nature of the activity? What should we understand when we call an activity urgent, important, or routine? Can activities be described only as urgent, important, and routine, or could there be combinations to describe a particular activity? This makes it necessary to understand the differentiations in greater detail.

An activity can be described as very important when the attainment of a goal depends directly upon it. It would be important if it contributes to the attainment of the goal, but does so indirectly. It would be less important if it contributes only to enhance the quality or perfection of the goal. And of course, it is unimportant if it does not affect the goal at all.

Urgency describes the relationship of the activity with time. It would be very urgent if the time were a critical factor. For example, a tax return must be filed before a particular date. Delayed filing attracts penalty. The activity would be urgent if, amongst others, time is an important criterion. When the deadline is not important, and the activity can be carried forward, it would be described as less urgent. For example, when audited accounts are to be filed with the Income Tax return on October 31, the activity of getting the accounts audited would be less urgent in April or May, because there is time to get it done later. If the time factor does not affect the goal, then it is certainly not urgent.

The next obvious question is how should we decide upon the priorities after we know the level of importance and urgency of a particular activity? To do this, give the first priority to whatever are both, important and urgent. The second on the priority list must be whatever is important. The third position must go to the activity that is urgent, and finally the fourth position goes to activities that have low importance and urgency. Initially, it may take a little time in differentiating the different activities, but with practice one soon becomes perfect in prioritising the activities.

Follow these simple steps to benefit from prioritising your activities:

1. Prepare a list of all the things that need to be done.
2. Mark each activity with A1, A2, A3 and A4 on the basis of their importance in attaining the goal.
3. Mark each activity with B1, B2, B3 and B4 on the basis of their urgency in attaining the goal.
4. On the basis of the markings, make a fresh list according to priorities assigned to the activities.
5. Can some of the activities be delegated to others? If so, do the needful.
6. Of the balance activities personally follow up on those of top priority. You will soon be attaining much more than what you have been doing earlier.

SAY "NO" TO INDECISION

One of the most important priorities in life is to take decisions at the right time. Taking a decision involves responsibility of having chosen between two or more options. Most people lack the confidence of taking a decision simply because of the criticism that may follow the choice of a wrong option. Putting off a decision reduces productivity. Besides, through repetition it becomes a bad habit. Take decisions as situations turn up. Follow these simple steps to take a decision:

1. Define the specific problem.
2. Collect all the relevant details and facts pertaining to the problem. Make appropriate allowance for a bias in the information received.
3. What are the possible solutions? Consider the pros and cons of each. Do not be influenced by external pressures.
4. Take the decision.

You will do well to remember that nobody takes all the right decisions. But those who take decisions regularly have a high percentage of correct decisions, as compared to those who do not take decisions. If you make a wrong decision, do not pass the blame to someone else. Accept your fault, and move on. The important thing to remember is that we gain experience from making mistakes.

SAY "NO" TO PROCRASTINATION

Procrastination has no place in the lives of people who want to get ahead. Every moment is precious. Just as indecision robs a person of productivity, so does procrastination. The truth is that indecision and procrastination are linked. We discussed it earlier, but we need to ensure that we do not have it in our lives. The truth is that people procrastinate because they *think* they are busy, or because they *think* the job is difficult. They also *think* that they do not like a particular job or activity, or because they are not up to it.

If procrastination bothers you, follow these simple ideas.

- Have a tent card on your worktable saying: DO IT NOW. Whenever, you begin to postpone an activity, the message will remind you of your weakness.
- When you find a particular assignment or activity appears difficult to be handled, break it into smaller segments. It makes it easier to handle. For example, you have been asked to prepare a comprehensive report about the sales activities of your competitor companies. You can break up the activity into several activities involving separate parties. Later, you could compile the facts and figures, and gradually refine the report over a few sittings.
- Tell yourself that it's important and urgent. Get down to it. When you are determined, nothing is difficult.
- Understand your own biorhythms. Tackle difficult jobs when your productivity levels are on a higher swing.

> **Think it over...**
>
> Never put off till tomorrow that which you can do today.
>
> — *Franklin*

YOUR PERSONAL LIFE

God has blessed you with life. Make the best of it. Wake up each morning with a positive attitude, ready to enjoy the many blessings He has showered upon you. In terms of time management, the utility time and leisure time are yours to enjoy. Many rush through their utility time, rushing through the bath and the meals. Is it worthwhile? If you cannot go through these necessities of life in comfort, when will you really appreciate 'life'? Have you really understood how enjoyable a good leisurely cup of tea or coffee can be? Do you know what it means to enjoy a special meal your wife may have especially cooked for you? Have you enjoyed the pleasure of a quiet meal in your favourite restaurant alone with your spouse? Many before you have rushed their way though life, hoping that some day they will get the time to enjoy life. Unfortunately, they never got the time. When they did, it was too late.

An important part of your personal life is the need to develop skills and abilities that become a part of your life as good habits. We discussed them earlier. Have you sincerely worked upon them? Let us review them again.

- Make self-improvement an important part of your goals in life. This will help you hone the existing skills and abilities, and also learn new ones. Keep up to date in your work by reading relevant trade journals.
- Read at least 12 books every year. Of these, four to six books should be on self-improvement subjects, and others could be leisure reading.
- Work to specific goals in every aspect of your life. Set long-term and short-term goals. These could be broken to annual, quarterly, monthly and weekly goals.
- Work one day at a time. Check your progress at the end of the day.
- Work on the basis of priorities every day. Differentiate between important, urgent, and routine work. Remember that 20 percent of the correct activities will contribute to 80 percent productivity.
- Review your goals and achievements periodically. If necessary, make changes in your plans to attain the set goals.

Leisure activities are just as important as one's work. These activities may not contribute financially like those at the workplace do, but they are a definite need in promoting relaxation and getting rid of stress. Your hobbies can be an important step in preparing you for additional skills, and also letting out steam to de-stress you. Those who wish to take shortcuts, rather than pursue a hobby, fall back upon smoking or chewing tobacco, or to liquor by way of consuming alcoholic drinks. In extreme cases people have taken use of drugs.

Hobbies may appear trifling to others. Some may even tell you that you are wasting your time. The truth is that these activities help de-stress, control fatigue, and recharge you mentally and emotionally. This promotes creative growth. Have a definite time for them in your time schedule.

Every individual needs moments of total silence, a time when the external world is cut off. These are the moments for quiet introspection. Rather than look externally, one needs to take a look within. These moments can be some of the best moments of one's life. Many prefer to spend them close to Nature in a garden or park, or besides a lake or river. A few even prefer to stroll through a lonely forest. Nature fortifies one's mind to appreciate the gifts of God, to release energy and creativity to enhance not only the productivity, but also the satisfaction one derives from life.

God plays an important part in the lives of many people, who derive still greater strength through prayer, devotion and faith. By instilling peace and happiness in the lives of people, they also enhance productivity and satisfaction.

Think it over...

The past and present are only our means; the future is always our end. Thus we never really live, but only hope to live. Always looking forward to being happy, it is inevitable that we should never be so.

— *Blaise Pascal*

YOUR FAMILY LIFE

The family is the purpose of all activity at the workplace and in the society. A family constitutes the basic institute on which all civilisation stands. In the Western countries, we can notice families, which are devoid of traditions and deep relationships, breaking, causing heartbreak, loneliness and depression. A large psychiatric workforce is helping people to find their bearings.

A materialistic way of life, centred on earning and flaunting money, is pushing many people towards the brink. To avoid such situations, it is important to remember that the family desires quality time more than money that most people have to offer. Therefore, it is important that in any time schedule there must be time for the spouse and the family. It is not enough to provide the luxuries and comforts of a home only. The family seeks quality time. Interaction with them is more important.

It is appreciated that the pressures of work prevent many people from interacting with their families in the way they would like to, but eating and praying together, helping the spouse and children within the home, watching common television programmes, going out together on weekends, or taking a short vacation, help cement relationships that last a lifetime. They are a part of a balanced life, and must find place in life goals.

When both the husband and wife are working, pressures increase within a home, particularly when there are children who need attention. Here are a few tried ideas that have helped ease pressure in the home:

- Let the children take the daily bath in the evening.
- Get the children to pack their school bags after completing the homework in the evening. Their school uniforms too could be got ready before bedtime.
- Some mothers even prefer to have the children's tiffin boxes ready in the evening, and place them in the refrigerator.
- You could plan ahead when guests are expected. Food items can be cooked and frozen, or stored in the refrigerator.
- Many housewives prepare tomato puree, onion-ginger-garlic mixture, boiled potatoes and items of frequent use in bulk, and store in a refrigerator.
- Housewives fond of cooking maintain personal recipe and cooking hints scrapbook.
- Many housewives plan a menu for the whole week to cater to the taste of everyone in the family.
- Teach the children to help you. This provides them training for adult life, and also reduces working pressures.
- Follow time management techniques like advance planning, making lists and using priorities.

EFFECTIVENESS AT THE WORKPLACE

Every day one spends almost 8 hours, or more, at work. During this time, one interacts with a variety of people within the workplace and outside. Some of these people may directly, or indirectly, affect the use of your time, and thereby your productivity or effectiveness.

What does one need to do to be effective at the workplace? Here are a few ideas that are known to have enhanced productivity.

- Have the office planned that it promotes productivity. It should be so planned that there is a natural sequence of activities, irrespective of their nature.
- Every person in the office must be clear about his or her responsibilities. While it is all right to give specific responsibilities to persons, but in the absence of one, the other should not let down the office activity.
- The ideal rule about office furniture, equipment, accessories and other requisites is that there must be a place assigned for everything. After use, the thing must return where it belongs. It is not unusual to find chairs, stools and crockery lying scattered in wrong places.
- Business is people. In any office, there will be people who will need to be attended to. Many of these will be important as customers and clients. There will be others who are intruders upon productive time. Screening is useful, but the important thing is who does the screening, and how.
- There must be definite rules about receiving visitors, responding to their inquiries, and guiding them to the right people in the shortest possible time, without

inconvenience to them, and without disturbing the workforce.

- In any office, there will be a lot of papers coming in, and going out. There must be a definite system for handling these papers in the least possible time. It is important that each of them goes to the concerned persons in the workforce, and is attended to according to their importance.
- The office must have a well-planned filing system, where documents are filed. The ideal system is one where a document can be retrieved in the least possible time.
- A good data bank is an asset in every office. Swift retrieval of information is the mark of an effective system.
- Sometimes meetings are necessary. However, a large majority is a waste of time. A definite system must be in place to ensure that meetings are called only when necessary, and that all meetings result in enhanced productivity.
- There must be definite system to ensure that the workforce arrives and leaves on time. The lunch and tea breaks should not be misutilised.

The most important thing that affects individual productivity in the office are one's personal working habits and attitudes. We have discussed these earlier. It is necessary that one must ensure that the working desk has no pending papers or files at the time of leaving office. They must return to their place. Most people have the habit of stuffing these into the desk drawers. If you do, ensure that they are disposed off the next day. At least once every month clear out your desk drawers, and throw away whatever is not necessary.

> **Think it over...**
>
> Lost wealth may be restored by industry, – the wreck of health regained by temperance, – forgotten knowledge restored by study, – alienate friendship smoothed into forgetfulness, – even forfeited reputation won by penitence and virtue. But who ever looked upon his vanished hours, – recalled his slighted years, – stamped them with wisdom, – or effaced from Heaven's record the fearful blot of wasted time?
>
> — *Lydia H. Sigourney*

YOU AND THE SOCIETY

Friendships are based upon an equal give-and-take basis. Many times this balance is not as equal, or delicate, as one would imagine it to be. Very often friends may impose requests on your time by way of invitations to weddings or parties. You may find it difficult to say "no". What should you do? What should be the criterion for a decision in such situations? Should your decision be work-oriented or friendship-oriented? The choice is yours. You will have to choose between saying "no", and sparing the time desired of you. You should try to strike a balance between the two. When you want to say "no", use words that express regret, words that express definite sentiments and explain the situation. The words must be polite and contain the reason. Never feel guilty about saying "no". You have a responsibility towards yourself and the family.

Besides the friends, there will be other pressures on your time. The housing society where you live will have certain expectations of you. Also the clubs you may have joined would desire a certain amount of participation from you. And what about the people who are a part of everyday life? The security guard who wishes as you leave or return to your building, the gardener who looks after the garden, or the liftman who carries you and the family up and down the building every day. Even the people you come across as a part of your professional activities have expectations of you. Each one of these activities places a certain demand on your time. This will mean making adjustments. Your personal attitude towards this expenditure of time is important. If you are positive, you will accept it as part of life, and find it satisfying. However, if you look at it as an unnecessary interruption in your life, it will be a cause of stress.

Just as we derive a lot of benefits from the society, it is equally important that we repay a part of the debt by giving some of our time to the society. Accept it as a part of life. Have enough flexibility in your life schedule to accommodate these little investments of time.

LIVE ONE DAY AT A TIME

We have discussed goals, both long-term and short-term. We have discussed how these goals can be attained through valid *Plans of Action*, focussed on each goal. We have discussed how we can attain satisfaction and happiness through a balanced life, which touches every aspect of life. It is good to derive experience and knowledge from whatever has gone by. It is equally essential to look at the future, to see where we are going. However, in the real essence, life must be lived one day at a time. It is of no use to look at our past with remorse for what we could not attain, or at the future for what we hope to achieve.

Every morning, God grants everyone another day that holds promise of giving the very best, without distinction of caste, colour or creed. It does not ask what religion you belong to, or what faith you follow. It does not even question your sex or age. It offers everyone another day of wholesome life. It is for you to decide how you wish to use it. If you want to be happy, enjoy every moment of your time, irrespective of where you are, or what you are doing. These happy moments will add on to give you joy, happiness and bliss. When it is time to leave this world, you can proudly say, "I invested my time well."

Think it over...

Time is that which in all things passes away; it is the form under which the will to live has revealed to it that its effects are in vain; it is the agent by which at every moment all things in our hands become as nothing, and lose all value.

— *Arthur Schopenhauer*

POINTS TO PONDER

- One must live a balanced life to be recognised as a successful person.
- Learn to convert the mistakes you make into valuable experience.

- No amount of emphasis on planning is enough. It is the basis of all success.
- If anything can go wrong, it will. Handle problems swiftly.
- Beware the time traitors. They will continue to lure and catch you off-guard throughout life.
- Explore your full potential by understanding your biorhythmic pattern.
- Avoid repetitive work. Try multi-tasking.
- Do not lavishly over-commit your time to others.
- Maintain a databank for future use.
- Whatever you do, work to priorities. Learn how to prioritise.
- Say “no” to indecision and procrastination.
- You owe yourself a good and satisfying personal life.
- Your family is the purpose of all activity at the workplace and the society.
- You can learn to be effective at the workplace.
- You owe some of your time to the society where you live.
- Live one day at a time, and be happy.

NOTES